Aspects of Language Teaching

H. G. Widdowson

Oxford University Press 1990

Oxford University Press
Walton Street, Oxford OX2 6DP

Oxford   New York   Toronto
Delhi   Bombay   Calcutta   Madras   Karachi
Petaling Jaya   Singapore   Hong Kong   Tokyo
Nairobi   Dar es Salaam   Cape Town
Melbourne   Auckland

and associated companies in
Berlin   Ibadan

Oxford, Oxford English and the *Oxford English logo* are trade
marks of Oxford University Press

ISBN 0 19 437128 X

Set in 10/12 pt Sabon.
Typeset by Pentacor Ltd, High Wycombe, Bucks.
Printed in Hong Kong.

In memory of Peter Strevens.

Contents

Acknowledgements

A number of the chapters of this book have developed from presentations at conferences and published papers. Chapter 2 started life as a plenary address at the 11th Annual Ontario TESL Conference in Toronto in November 1983. Chapters 3 and 4 grew out of a paper originally commissioned by the Council of Europe and submitted in September 1986. An earlier version of Chapter 6 was read at the Fifth National LEND conference in Rimini in November 1985, and appeared in print in a collection of papers edited by William Rutherford and Michael Sharwood-Smith entitled *Grammar and Second Language Teaching* published by Newbury House in 1988. Chapter 9 is an elaboration of a paper written for a book called *Language Syllabuses: The State of the Art* edited by M L Tickoo and published in 1987 by the Regional English Language Centre in Singapore. Parts of Chapter 10 began as a presentation entitled *Design Principles for a Communicative Grammar*, given at a TESOL symposium and subsequently published in an ELT Document (124) edited by Christopher Brumfit. The original for Chapter 11 was a plenary address at the IATEFL Annual Conference in Brighton, April 1986. It was published in *English Language Teaching Journal* Volume 41, Number 2 just one year later.

I am grateful to all those people who have given me the opportunity to make my thoughts public in talk and print.

I would like to express my appreciation, too, to all those colleagues and students who have stimulated and guided my thinking over the years by pertinent observation and critical comment and who have supported me, more than they know, by their approval and the sense of community that they provide. I should like to make particular mention of Simon Murison-Bowie, not only because of the valuable comments he made on an earlier draft of this book, but also for twenty years of companionship in the profession.

The content of this book, then, owes a great deal to the ideas of many other people. Its compilation owes a great deal to one person, Sybil Spence. For her unfailing patience, dedication and care in preparing copy for publication I am extremely grateful.

Acknowledgements are made to the following publishers from whose texts the extracts and diagrams below have been taken:

Ann Brumfit and Scott Windeatt, *Communicative Grammar 2 and 3* (ELTA/OUP 1984)

Emily Dickinson, *Selected Poems of Emily Dickinson*, ed. Conrad Aiken (Random House, The Modern Library: New York 1924)

W. Somerset Maugham, 'The Unconquered', *Complete Short Stories* (Heinemann 1951)

Preface

This book has been made out of a number of papers written over the past five years or so. Most of them were originally prepared as conference presentations, some appeared subsequently in print. My first intention was simply to put them together as a compilation with a minimum of additional comment. Then I saw that there were matters which called for further expounding and for explicit cross-reference. So I went to work elaborating and linking. The papers grew into chapters. And as chapters, they carry the implicit claim that they constitute parts of a reasonably coherent and uniform whole.

But this manner of composition leaves its traces. The original papers were designed for particular occasions and purposes as self-contained statements. Certain ideas and arguments naturally appear therefore in several places, variously emphasized and formulated as appropriate to the perspectives of different discussions. When the papers are brought together and fashioned as chapters they cease to be separate episodes and become elements in a sequence. While recurrence is necessary for the independence of each paper as such, when it appears in chapters, which are linked in *inter*dependent continuity, it can read like needless repetition. What I have done is to pare away some of the repetition while retaining recurrence where I feel it is necessary to restate ideas in demonstration of their more specific relevance to the chapters concerned.

The chapters are assembled into three parts, each of which deals with a central theme. The first of these perhaps calls for particular comment because it sets the key, so to speak, for the discussion in the rest of the book. In it I enquire into the nature of language teaching as a professional enterprise. What does the process of teaching actually involve? What do teachers need to know in theory and what procedures do they need to employ in practice to actualize that knowledge as effective action? How can they learn from experience? These questions have to do with the education of teachers and their status as professional people. They are questions which I have raised on occasions elsewhere, but I make no apology for giving them prominence here. They take precedence over all others within the scope of this book. Unless they are seriously considered, proposals for general curriculum change or particular classroom techniques are effectively meaningless, for such proposals have to be mediated by teachers and such mediation presupposes a degree of awareness and expertise which only a thoroughgoing and continuing teacher education can provide.

This might seem an obvious point, but it is one which those responsible for determining current educational policy in Britain, for example, seem to have some difficulty in grasping. They are busy planning a National Curriculum which necessarily requires a degree of professionalism for which little provision is being made. Teachers tend to be referred to as if they were factory workers to be provided with minimal practical skills and required to pick up on the job whatever extra expertise is necessary to keep the pedagogic production line going. The result is that teachers' morale declines with their status. Many leave a profession officially treated with such disdain. Furthermore, expedient stop-gap attempts to provide for the lack of qualified teachers only make matters worse. I read in my newspaper today (6 July 1989), for example, of a teacher with only rudimentary French and no German being engaged to teach both languages in a secondary school. I read that it has been calculated that 25 per cent of teaching in British secondary schools is being carried out by teachers with an inadequate knowledge of the subject. Those in authority seem not to be particularly troubled by this situation. So long as there are people available to stand in front of classes it does not seem to matter very much about their competence as teachers. If it is expedient and cheap to employ licensed teachers rather than qualified ones then this solution will be preferred whatever the consequences for education.

In the light of such attitudes it is particularly important to assert the professional status of teaching. But the assertion of status has to be supported by a corresponding commitment on the part of teachers to standards of professionalism. These standards, as I argue in Part 1, depend on a continual process of self-education through an evaluation of practice in reference to theory. Unless teaching is informed by principled pragmatism in this way, it can make no claim to be a serious professional activity. It becomes hack work. I would argue that teachers who reject theory as being irrelevant to practice not only misunderstand the nature of their work, but at the same time undermine the profession. Furthermore they lend support in this way to the enemies of education and so ultimately act against their own interests.

Part 1, then, investigates the nature of language teaching in general as a principled professional activity. It deals with the interdependence of theory and practice and the appropriate exploitation of ideas. Part 2 then looks at one theoretical area which it seems reasonable to suppose is relevant to language teaching, namely enquiries into the nature of language. Here I look at the relationship between words, grammar, and context, at how meaning is encoded semantically within the linguistic system on the one hand and achieved pragmatically by contextual negotiation on the other. I then seek to show in Part 3 how these perspectives on language description lead to different approaches to the teaching of language. Thus Parts 2 and 3 are intended to exemplify the kind of critical enquiry which, as I argue in Part 1, should direct the work of language teachers. I say the *kind* of critical enquiry. It would run counter to my own position to suggest that the teachers' professional salvation depends on their accepting the ideas and arguments proposed in these pages.

For the validity of ideas and arguments is always relative. To begin with, whether they are acceptable or not will depend on the extent to which one accepts beliefs of a general ideological kind on which they are based. I have already expressed one belief of this sort, namely that to deny the relevance of theory is unprofessional practice. If readers do not accept this belief there is no point in their reading this book—or any other book on the principles of language teaching. There are two other and related beliefs which direct the thinking of these chapters and, by the same token, limit their validity for other minds. It would be as well for me to make them explicit too.

First there is the belief in the importance of analytic thought. It seems to me that it is the purpose of education (teacher education included) to develop ways of applying the intellect to experience, of pushing rational enquiry as far as it will go. This is not to deny the value of experience but only to say that this value is not intrinsic to experience itself but is derived from it by reflection. Experience, one might say, is the sensation which the mind must make sense of. It provides the data for analysis. This should not be taken to mean that all experience is explicable by reference to reason. Heaven forbid that this should be so. But we can only really tell what is genuinely inexplicable when explanation fails. To accept that something is mysterious and beyond the reach of reason before trying to subject it to rational analysis is simply to diminish the mystery and make it commonplace. So, in reference to this book, one can acknowledge that there are aspects of language teaching which will remain mysterious, that, in the last analysis, teaching is an art depending on the intuitive flair of individual personalities. In the last analysis, agreed: for it is only as a consequence of analysis that one can arrive at such a conclusion. Of course, there will be differences of opinion about which aspects of teaching should be analysed and about the validity of the analysis. All enquiry, as I have said, is limited by preconceived assumptions, and readers are likely to have some of their own which are at variance with mine. That is all to the good. Readers may then be induced to review their own position by the kind of critical thinking it is the purpose of this book to provoke.

Finally, much of the argument in this book is based on a belief in the need for preconceived ideas as a condition for effective language teaching and learning. Teaching and learning: the order is significant. For the preconceived ideas are used by the teacher to control the learning process. They define pedagogic principles. This view is not, I know, a popular one. The notion of teacher control is anathema in many quarters. It sounds illiberal. It smacks of prescription and even perhaps suggests the suppresion of human rights. The view which prevails in many places is one which holds that the description of language use and the promotion of language learning should proceed *without* preconceived ideas, because otherwise the language behaviour of real people, users and learners, is cramped into conformity and so misrepresented on the one hand, inhibited on the other. Instead, it is argued, we should let the people speak, as it were, for themselves. If they are learners we should let them find their own natural way as they go, instead of confining them to an itinerary fixed in advance. This is a seductive doctrine and one of which it would be wise to be wary. As I have already suggested, all enquiry presupposes a purpose of one sort or another and so is primed by a set of ideas. Otherwise, there is no way in which one can make sense of experience. Language learning is no different. There must always be some points of reference to give direction to the process and it is the teachers' task to provide them. The idea that learners will learn efficiently for themselves if they are left alone is, I believe, misconceived. If natural learning was so effective there would be no need for education at all. Classrooms exist to provide opportunities which would otherwise be denied by controlling conditions for learning which would not otherwise take place. Pedagogy presupposes control and control presupposes preconceived ideas. The central question is how this control is to be exercised tactically, tightened, or relaxed so as to facilitate the learning process: how preconceived ideas are to be evaluated and modified to accommodate unpredictable developments in the classroom. It is when control is inflexible and ideas fixed that they become constraints on learning. Otherwise they are necessary conditions. It is in the setting up of such conditions that teachers apply their special knowledge and expertise and discharge their professional responsibility.

It is because learners do not learn effectively without the intervention of properly educated teachers that we need to insist on the proper professional standards and status of teaching. It is to those who take the profession of language teaching seriously in this way that this book is addressed and dedicated.

HGW
London, July 1989

Note
On the matter of controversial pronominals, I have either sought to avoid them by plurality, or to imply dual or neutral reference by the random distribution of *he, she*, and so on. If I have lapsed I can only hope that readers will neutrally eke out my imperfections with their thoughts.

PART ONE

The theory and practice of language teaching

1   Introduction

General matters of principle

The purpose of this first part of the book is to establish a perspective on language teaching. It provides a conceptual setting for what follows in the succeeding chapters.

This perspective aims to present teaching as a self-conscious enquiring enterprise whereby classroom activities are referred to theoretical principles of one sort or another. These principles essentially define the subject: they are the bearings that teachers need to take in order to plot their course. The theory which provides such bearings may come from a variety of sources: from experience or experiment, from sudden inspirational insight, from the archives of conventional wisdom. But wherever it comes from, the theory needs to be made explicit and public if its relevance to pedagogy is to be effectively assessed.

This is not to deny that individual teachers may be highly effective in making their own way by an intuitive sense of direction. The effectiveness of teaching cannot be equated with its rational accountability. In any classroom there will always be aspects of the classroom encounter, the play of personality, the tactics of expedient interaction, which will defy the reduction to generality.

But if we are to talk about pedagogy, individual effort must be referred to more general ideas, otherwise there is no way for experience to be communicated, no way in which others can derive benefit from the particular successes of the individual. What principles do is to make private experience publicly accessible, open to discussion and capable of wider relevance. In our case, they enable us to claim that there is indeed a pedagogy of language teaching and a profession which practises it.

So an insistence on the importance of principle in no way denies the value of experience or customary practices but simply requires that they are subjected to evaluation, and not just taken

on trust. Experience of itself has no significance but can only
have significance attributed to it. Custom of itself is no surety of
effective action. It may of course turn out that there are after all
good independent reasons for respecting the intuitive judgements which come from long experience. But it does not seem
sensible to accept them unless they can be given rational
sanction. The contexts of language teaching, like the more
general social contexts within which they are located, are
continually changing, continually challenging habitual ways of
thinking and the patterns of past certainty. Unless there is a
corresponding process of critical appraisal, there can be no
adaptation, no adjustment to change.

Principle and technique

Principles are abstractions. They have to be actualized as
techniques in the particular circumstances of different classrooms. The teaching task is to see that the techniques that are
used are effective in promoting learning objectives, so they have
to be designed to account for specific contexts of instruction. A
technique may be consistent with a principle but ineffective for a
particular group of learners. This may be a case of inadequate
actualization, and this would call for a change of technique. On
the other hand, of course, it may be that the principle itself needs
to be questioned. How can the teachers tell?

The teachers' dilemma is the same as that of the researcher
outside the classroom. The researcher has a hypothesis and sets
up experiments to test it. If these do not yield results which
support the hypothesis, it may either be because the experiments
were ineffectively designed, in which case the researcher will
design some more, or because the hypothesis was invalid as
formulated in the first place, in which case the researcher will
reformulate it, and then work out what new experiments are
needed to test it. Language teachers can be seen as involved in
very much the same sort of process—their principles correspond
to hypotheses, their techniques to experiments. Teachers too are
faced with methodological decisions as to where adjustments are
to be made in the matching up of abstraction with actuality.

Teaching as a research activity

Teaching, then, can be conceived of as a research activity

whereby experimental techniques of instruction are designed to correspond with hypothetical principles of pedagogy, with provision made for mutual adjustment so as to bring validity of principle into as close an alignment as possible with the utility of technique.

But of course teachers have extra commitments. They cannot just assume the researcher role and use students as experimental subjects, observing how they learn under varying conditions with detached interest to satisfy an intellectual curiosity. The teacher's business is to *induce* learning and the techniques that are used have to work to that end. In effect, teachers become intervening variables in their own experiments. Their research has to be applied in the very process of enquiry: it has to be directly accountable in terms of practical pay-off.

This being so, we can regard the classroom as the context for two related kinds of activity. In one, techniques are devised with regard to their practical effectiveness in the promotion of learning. They are directed at the benefit of learners. This we might call the instructional activity, with the teacher engaged as participant mediating the techniques concerned. In the other activity, techniques are related to principles with a view to enquiring into the relationship between the two. Here they are directed at the benefit of the teachers' own understanding of their craft. This we might call the experimental activity, with the teacher acting as observer manipulating the techniques concerned.

Thus the experimental activity and the instructional activity are reciprocally enhanced, and the most effective pedagogy is one in which the two act together, each informing and reinforcing the other. In this way, teaching which provides for learner development serves the cause of teacher development at the same time. It fulfils a dual educational purpose.

The view of pedagogy proposed here, then, makes teachers responsible for defining their own problems and providing their own solutions. Research from outside, whether descriptive, experimental or speculative, cannot therefore be directly transposed to the classroom context. It does, however, have a crucial role to play in two respects, theoretically and methodologically. Theoretically, it can serve as a source of ideas and insights which are of potential relevance for the formulation of principles: ideas emerging from disciplines devoted to the study of language and learning which might bear upon the definition of language as subject. Methodologically, it can provide precept and example of what is involved in critical enquiry, of how intuition can be subjected to conceptual and empirical evaluation. It can raise consciousness of the whole process of continuing self-appraisal.

Some people will perhaps feel uneasy about the definition of pedagogy as operational research in which experience is pressed into partnership with principled enquiry. It may seem too much like confinement, a denial of individual enterprise and the constraining of intuition into patterns of conformity. It looks as if it might cramp the teacher's style. This raises an issue which is of general relevance to the matters discussed in this book. It has to do with the relationship between individual initiative and conventional constraint, with the limits social conditions put on the freedom of thought and action. This is, of course, an issue of much wider social and political significance which it is not part of my brief to explore. But it finds expression in current ideas and attitudes within the theoretical and practical domains of language study, language teaching and language teacher education. Since these *are* within my brief in this book, the issue warrants consideration here.

The limits of initiative

In very general terms, what has characterized recent tendencies in the theoretical study and the practical teaching of language has been a distrust of authority and of the rules and conventions through which it is exercised. Thus in the theoretical study of language the deference previously accorded to analysis and explanation by the informed observer has been questioned in favour of an uncommitted approach to enquiry, without preconception and without privilege, into the ways in which participants negotiate their own conditions for achieving their purposes. And in language teaching, the idea that the teacher should direct the progress of learners has been questioned on the grounds that such direction impedes the natural process of learning. In both theoretical and practical domains, therefore, the exercise of authority is seen to result in the artificial manipulation of the actuality of experience. The description of language use is thereby distorted. The development of language learning is thereby disrupted.

While acknowledging the danger of ideas casting reality in their own image and serving the cause of suppression, one needs to be wary, it seems to me, of being too readily persuaded by the heady vision of individual freedom which these tendencies invoke. To begin with, one can discern in this thinking some confusion between what is *authoritative* and what is *authoritarian*, and to suppose that because some preconceptions are used' in the exercise of power, all preconceptions, no matter how conceived, and no matter how prudently used, are to be rejected out of hand.

There is here, I believe, a fundamental misunderstanding about the nature of knowledge and learning. For these are, of their very nature, dependent on the acknowledgement of existing conceptual frameworks. Their definition presupposes delimitation. To know is to have formulated experience in reference to given categories; to learn is to engage in the process of such formulation. To be sure, these categories are not inscribed immutably in the mind: they can be altered to accommodate new experience. But they cannot be altered unless they are first apprehended. What is new is only recognizable in relation to what is given, individual inspiration only recognizable in relation to accepted social convention. The freedom of independent initiative only exists as a meaningful notion if there are limits to define it. So the rules and conventions which set these limits are effectively, if paradoxically, the surest guarantee we have of freedom of thought and action. They operate negatively as constraints, but positively as enabling conditions.

The central question, then, is not whether or not we should tolerate the rules and conventions, the systems of thought, the preconceptions that regulate enquiry and instruction—for if our enterprise is to have any significance at all we have to—but *which* rules, conventions, and preconceptions are likely to offer us the most relevant and reliable set of bearings for our work, and *how* we are to use them so that we can allow for their modification, or even their complete replacement, when new insights and experiences need to be accommodated. The identification of appropriate preconceptions is precisely the recognition of hypothetical principles I referred to earlier: and their effective actualization in practice is a matter of experimental technique.

Applied linguistics

The mediation between theory and practice that I have been

discussing here defines the domain of applied linguistics as this relates to language teaching.

Its scope delimited in this way, applied linguistics is in my view an activity which seeks to identify, within the disciplines concerned with language and learning, those insights and procedures of enquiry which are relevant for the formulation of pedagogic principles and their effective actualization in practice (Widdowson 1979, 1984a). In effect what applied linguistics does is to enquire into cross-cultural accommodation: it transfers ideas and methods from different disciplinary cultures and seeks to demonstrate how they can be made coherent and effective in the different conditions of pedagogic practice. Some people involved in this enterprise concentrate on making ideas coherent; others focus attention on their relationship with data; some speculate, and some experiment, and some do both. But these efforts are of no eventual pedagogic value unless they can be carried through into the classroom context. Applied linguistics in this sense must be practised by teachers too if it is to have any effective operational relevance at all. If applied linguistics is left exclusively to an elite band of researchers, then the whole object of the exercise disappears.

The perspective on pedagogy that informs this book, then, makes considerable demands on the practising teacher. But these are no greater than are required to substantiate a claim to professional status. And while they charge the teacher with more responsibility than has sometimes been customary in the past, they also bring corresponding rewards in the way of job satisfaction and self-esteem.

2 Problems with solutions

From the perspective outlined in the preceding chapter, language teaching can be seen as a principled problem-solving activity: a kind of operational research which works out solutions to its own local problems. But it is not always seen in this way. There is a very pervasive belief that it is research in theoretical and applied linguistics which provides the solutions. My view would be that it does nothing of the sort and that if we think it does we delude ourselves. Disciplinary research has a role, but it is not as a purveyor of solutions. Much of it is engrossed with problems internally generated within the research itself, sometimes because of the need for experimental precision, sometimes because of conceptual ineptitude. But I am running on too fast. Let me approach the theme of this chapter more circumspectly by way of literary reference.

Samuel Johnson, a notable figure in the field of language study, took upon himself the task of compiling a dictionary of the English language. One of the problems of lexicography, as he recognized, is how to provide explanations of words by the use of other words whose meanings are self-evident. As Johnson himself put it in his Preface:

> To explain, requires the use of terms less abstruse than that which is to be explained, and such terms cannot always be found; for as nothing can be proved but by supposing something intuitively known, and evident without proof, so nothing can be defined but by the use of words too plain to admit a definition.

The use of simple terms to meet the purpose of a dictionary as a work of reference for the general public can, however, conflict with semantic precision. Not all of the entries in Johnson's dictionary conform to this principle of plainness. Here, for example, is the definition of the word *network*:

NETWORK: Any thing reticulated or decussated, at equal distances, with interstices between the intersections.

How do we account for this obfuscation? It seems clear that what has happened here is that Johnson has forgotten about the problem of finding ways of making meaning plain and has shifted to a different lexicographical problem, namely how to provide an exhaustive definition of words so that their entire meaning is made explicit. In seeking to solve this second problem of semantic exactitude, he not only fails to solve the problem of making meanings plain to the public but actually makes that problem a good deal more complex.

The matching of solution to problem

What I want to point out by this example is that the nature of a solution is determined by the prior definition of the problem that goes with it. Problem and solution are a kind of conceptual adjacency pair, comparable with question and answer in conversation. It makes no more sense to talk about solutions without being absolutely clear about what problems they solve, than it does to talk about excellent answers to questions that have never been posed. Solutions presuppose problems as answers presuppose questions, as the sentence (in the legal sense) presupposes a verdict. 'Sentence first, verdict afterwards,' cries the Red Queen in *Alice in Wonderland*. However, this is not the acceptable order in our ordinary world.

But surely all this, you may say, is self-evident. That may be so, but it does not prevent people in our field from continually falling into the error of supposing that a solution designed to match one problem must be applicable to quite a different problem as well. Let us consider a few cases.

Case 1: Linguistics

A linguist devises a model of grammar in the process of developing a theory of human cognition. Among those concerned with language teaching some assume that such a model must also be directly relevant to problems of pedagogy, that in general the principles and objectives which define the *discipline* of linguistics must necessarily also apply to the *subject* of language teaching in the school curriculum. Others assume that such theoretical enquiry can have no relevance whatever. Neither position is tenable.

We cannot assume that what the linguist identifies as significant should correspond with aspects of language to be focused on in the teaching and learning of a language as a school subject. But this is not of course to deny that relevance or significance can be inferred, that insights can be drawn from the discipline and their implications for the subject explored. Indeed as I have suggested in Chapter 1, it can be seen as the business of applied linguistics to do just this. But the linguist cannot determine relevance.

Chomsky, the linguist referred to here, recognizes this. He has expressed scepticism about the significance of linguistics for language teaching. But since he acknowledges that he has no expertise in the field of language teaching, there is no reason to take his remarks as authoritative. They do, however, raise issues that have a direct bearing on the theme of this part of the book and are worth quoting at some length:

> I should like to make it clear from the outset that I am participating in this conference not as an expert on any aspect of the teaching of languages, but rather as someone whose primary concern is with the structure of language and, more generally, the nature of cognitive processes.
>
> Furthermore I am, frankly, rather sceptical about the significance, for the teaching of languages, of such insights and understanding as have been attained by linguistics and psychology. Certainly the teacher of language would do well to keep informed of progress and discussions in these fields, and the efforts of linguists and psychologists *to approach the problems of language teaching from a principled point of view* are extremely worthwhile, from an intellectual as well as a social point of view. Still, it is difficult to believe that either linguistics or psychology has achieved a level of theoretical understanding that might enable it to support *a 'technology' of language teaching*. Both fields have made significant progress in recent decades, and, furthermore, both draw on centuries of careful thought and study. These disciplines are, at present, in a state of flux and agitation. What seemed to be well-established doctrine a few years ago may now be the subject of extensive debate. Although it would be difficult to document the generalisation, it seems to me that there has been a significant decline, over the past ten or fifteen years, in the degree of confidence in the scope and security of foundations in both psychology and linguistics. I personally

feel that this decline in confidence is both healthy and realistic. But it should serve as a warning to teachers that suggestions from the 'fundamental disciplines' must be viewed with caution and scepticism. *(Chomsky 1965, quoted in Allen and van Buren 1971 [my italics])*

These remarks of Chomsky have often been quoted, and adduced more often than not, almost gleefully at times, as evidence in support of the view that linguistics has no relevance to language teaching and that therefore applied linguistics, as it relates to pedagogy at least, is vacuous. But if one troubles to read what Chomsky actually says here, it is apparent that he recognizes that linguistics and psychology are associated with ways of approaching 'the problems of language teaching from a principled point of view'. What he questions is whether these disciplines can 'support a "technology" of language teaching', that is to say, presumably, whether they can directly inform pedagogic technique.

I see Chomsky's position as consistent with the view I expressed earlier, namely that the theoretical disciplines provide a reference for establishing *principles* of approach, but they cannot determine *techniques*. So 'suggestions from the "fundamental disciplines" must be viewed with caution and scepticism'. This is very different from disregarding them altogether. What Chomsky is indicating, it seems to me, is that the significance of these disciplines is debatable: their relevance has to be demonstrated.

One might (in passing) compare Chomsky's comments, which raise issues it is 'healthy and realistic' to debate, with the following declaration of prejudice which simply pronounces the dogma that there are no issues worth debating:

I do not believe that linguistics has any contribution to make to the teaching of English or the standard European languages. The many people who claim that it has seem to me to deceive themselves and others. *(Sampson 1980: 10)*

Sampson, of course, has no more claim to authority on pedagogic matters than Chomsky does. The difference is that Chomsky acknowledges this fact and accordingly expresses his views with appropriate caution. Sampson, on the other hand, does not seem to feel in the least inhibited by his own lack of competence to pronounce on the matter.

Case 2: *Behaviourist psychology*

A psychologist develops an approach to the shaping of animal behaviour and demonstrates its effectiveness on rats and pigeons and then takes the reckless step of assuming that similar solutions apply to human behaviour. Language teachers, impressed by the apparent authority of science, follow suit and try to teach by means of operant conditioning. The solution shifts from pigeons to people in general to pupils in particular. I refer here, of course, to B. F. Skinner, whose views on language learning as essentially a matter of behaviour being shaped by stimulus control provided theoretical warrant for an approach to language teaching which focused on habit formation. The extreme positivist version of behaviourism which Skinner propounded was effectively demolished by Chomsky in his review of *Verbal Behaviour* (Chomsky 1959 in Allen & van Buren 1971: 136–9, 147–8). In current pedagogic fashion, behaviourist practices have been largely superseded by cognitive and communicative perspectives on learning. As a result, there is now a widespread supposition that there is nothing whatever of any theoretical validity or pedagogic value in behaviourist thinking. Its day is done: another day has dawned. Again we see how much easier it is to be absolute in allegiance to a doctrine rather than to enquire into the beliefs upon which it is founded. (For the kind of reasoned enquiry needed into the relevance of behaviourist ideas to language teaching see Rivers 1964.)

Total rejection of behaviourist theory is no more reasonable than total acceptance. For when one considers the matter, it is clear that there must be some aspects of language learning which have to do with habit formation. Effective communication depends on the immediate and automatic access to linguistic forms so that the mind can consciously engage in the more creative business of negotiating meaning. If these forms were not internalized as habitual mental patterns independent of thought, they could not be readily accessed and language could not function effectively as a means of thinking and communicating. It is just this point that is made by Lado, whose approach to language teaching is so often represented as directly opposed to the development of communicative abilities:

> Nothing could be more enslaving and therefore less worthy of the human mind than to have it chained to the mechanics of

the patterns of the language rather than free to dwell on the message conveyed through the language. It is precisely because of this view that we discover the highest purpose of PAT-TERN PRACTICE: TO REDUCE TO HABIT WHAT RIGHTFULLY BELONGS TO HABIT IN THE NEW LAN-GUAGE, so that the mind and personality may be freed to dwell in their proper realm, that is on the meaning of the communication rather than the mechanics of grammar. (*Lado 1957*)

Just *how* these habitual patterns are to be internalized for easy access is another matter: direct inducement by repetitive drill may well not be the best way, in which case the thing to do is to think of other techniques. But this does not entail an absolute denial of the principle. However, the tendency has been to assume that if behaviourist notions cannot account for *all* aspects of language learning it cannot account for *any*. Both the uncritical acceptance of Skinner's concept of the problem and solution of learning and its equally uncritical rejection in favour of another serve only to bring pedagogy into disrepute.

Case 3:   *The Threshold Level*

A group of experts in Europe set out to solve problems to do with language learning in continuing education for adults beyond formal schooling. Their proposed solutions are trans-ferred to schools in Europe and subsequently to schools everywhere else, and notional/functional syllabuses are peddled as nostrums all over the place as suitable for every situation.

I am referring to the work of the Council of Europe (see Trim *et al.* 1980). This has been an important influence in promoting a communicative approach to the teaching of languages. It should be noted, however, that the rationale for such an approach relates primarily to the ends and not the means of learning, and is directed at furthering the cause of cultural co-operation in Europe. The original concern for out-of-school education is evident in the way objectives are defined in terms of utility: threshold level specifications are drawn up with an eye to meeting the needs of learners as eventual participants in contexts of communicative interaction, rather than with a concern to activate the actual learning process itself. Their relevance outside the situation for which they were designed, where eventual aims cannot be so readily related to learning objectives, should not therefore be taken on trust (see Widdowson 1983). But it has been commonly supposed that specifications along threshold level lines must be universally relevant, without reference to the definition of objectives for learning on which the original threshold level specifications are based. Thus conclusions are adopted without a consideration of the local validity of the rationale from which they derive.

Case 4:   Humanistic learning

If people learn by caring and sharing and linking hands in Southern California, it does not follow they will learn by similar therapeutic techniques in Thailand and Tanzania. I refer here to so-called humanistic approaches to language teaching, and make specific allusion to Gertrude Moskowitz's book *Caring and Sharing in the Foreign Language Classroom* (1978). In contrast with the Council of Europe proposals, which seek to specify what learners are meant to achieve and so bear mainly upon questions relating to syllabus design, humanistic approaches are centrally concerned with the actual process of learning and therefore have a bearing primarily on methodology. (For a perceptive review, see Brumfit 1985: 79–95.)

The main aim of humanistic approaches is to draw the learner into an affective engagement with the learning process, to make classroom activities meaningful as experiences which involve the individual as a whole person. They serve as a valuable corrective to approaches of the kind that a behaviourist view might encourage, approaches which impose conformity on learners, reduce the scope of their participation as persons, and deny them the exercise of individual initiative in the learning process. However, it is not always recognized that individuality is itself a cultural concept: there can be no private independent real person dissociated from the cultural values which define the society in which the individual lives.

Furthermore, the individual may not *want* to reveal his private life in a public role. Thus, encouraging learners to explore and share their own personality can actually be seen as an unwarranted intrusion on privacy, and as the imposition of alien attitudes, in some cultures and for some individuals. In which case, it may lead to a *dis*engagement from learning. Activities which may resolve problems in one cultural (and therefore educational) setting may create problems in another. Pedagogy in this case actually makes the learning task more difficult.

It is also worth nothing, I think, that although 'whole-person', 'humanistic' approaches seem superficially to be opposed to behaviourism in their recognition of the individual's personality, on closer inspection the two views on learning seem in one fundamental respect to be essentially alike. Both focus on affective rather than cognitive factors as central to the process. One of the main tenets of behaviourism is that behaviour can be shaped through reinforcement by reward. Thus pigeons learn patterns of pecking behaviour by being given grain; students learn patterns of language behaviour by being given approval. In both cases acceptable responses are reinforced and learning is controlled by *affective regulation*. In the 'humanistic' view, learning is also brought about by the promotion of experiential well-being, but in this case by affective *self*-regulation.

What is underrated in both views is the cognitive dimension. Regulation can after all be a matter of acting on positive or negative evidence, the adjustment of behaviour by reference to feedback information. This evidence and adjustment can be quite free of affective associations. What we have here is *cognitive regulation*. Both behaviourism and 'humanistic' views would have us believe that to be affective is to be effective in setting up conditions for learning. But such a simple formula really will not do.

Case 5:   Immersion

If children become bilingual by being immersed in French in Canada, then perhaps all we need to do is to immerse Chinese-speaking children in English in Hong Kong to achieve the same effect. Immersion in this view would seem to be a kind of baptism which mysteriously induces the gift of tongues.

The immersion programme in Canada (described in Stern 1978, 1983; Swain 1978, 1982; Swain and Lapkin 1981) involves the teaching of French contingently by using it as a medium of instruction for other subjects on the curriculum. It can be seen as applying principles of ESP to the general curriculum of school education, presenting language as a service for the achievement of other than language objectives. It puts into operation on a more comprehensive scale a proposal for English teaching pedagogy that I myself put forward, speculatively, as appropriate for the Indian context (Widdowson 1968). How far it would be appropriate to the Hong Kong context I do not know. The point is that it cannot be *presumed* to be, without careful enquiry into the whole range of factors that bear upon educational decisions. Stern, one of those most closely concerned with the Canadian immersion programme, sounds a suitably cautionary note in respect to some of these factors:

> Efforts to create bilingualism by means of bilingual schooling —as, for example, in the immersion programme in Canada— are likely to be more successful than conventional language teaching as a subject because the language is treated in school as a medium rather than as a subject. But even in these cases the success is likely to be shortlived if it is not backed by bilingual contacts and exchanges in the community at large. Thus, the success of language teaching is dependent upon major forces in society, such as the role, or perception of, language in that society. *(Stern 1983:426)*

It should also be noted that the success of such immersion by medium teaching is not complete. Students appear to acquire more in the way of fluency than accuracy:

> There is evidence to show that after six to seven years of an immersion program, productive use of the second language still differs considerably in grammatical and lexical ways from that of native speakers. *(Harley and Swain 1984: 291)*

It would seem that students need something in the way of formal instruction as well as acquisition by natural exposure and engagement. It is not just that one supplements the other: effective learning would appear to be a function of the *relationship* between formal instructional and natural use.

> Learners require opportunities for both form-focused and function-focused practice in the development of particular skill areas, and if one or the other is lacking they do not appear to benefit as much ... Learners who live in what Krashen has referred to as 'acquisition-rich' environments and take advantage of such settings to use their communicative skills in the L2, also need opportunities to focus on the functional properties of the language and attend to form. *(Spada 1985: 22–3. See also Spada 1987)*

All this would seem to cast some doubt on the idea that in

using the language for communicative purposes, the learner automatically and without other instruction internalizes the detailed knowledge of language as a generative system available for general use.

The problem of empirical evidence: an example

Surrounded as we are by solutions of all kinds, each one supported by persuasive evidence of attested success, we cannot but be tempted into the belief that somewhere among them there will be one which matches our particular teaching problem, and which can therefore be slotted into our situation like a cassette or a computer programme. But this is a temptation which should be strenuously resisted. One must beware especially of solutions that are presented as if they were based on the results of rigorous experimental tests and bear the stamp of proof.

Consider how easy it is to be misled by the persuasive power of apparent proof. A group of researchers wish to find out whether there is any substance in the idea that second language learners follow a natural predetermined path in their internalization of the language system they are learning. A test is devised, known as the Bilingual Syntax Measure (see Burt, Dulay, and Hernandez 1973), which will require an appropriate number of subjects to provide certain linguistic responses by reference to pictures. These responses are then examined to see how the subjects perform on the production of certain given morphemes (the progressive morpheme -*ing*, the plural morpheme, the past tense morpheme, etc.) in linguistic contexts which would, in native speaker speech, require their obligatory occurrence.

Now by looking at how the subjects perform on these tests, our researcher will be able to determine different degrees of accuracy for each of the morphemes focused upon in this way. Thus it might be established that the progressive -*ing* has a high accuracy rating and the past tense morpheme -*ed* a low one, that the plural morpheme -*s* rates high on this accuracy measure as compared with the singular third person morpheme -*s*, and so on. An interesting finding. But we will suppose that our researcher is cautious in making claims, and so might wish to extend the enquiry and see whether the same results can be replicated with different subjects doing different tasks. After all, this accuracy order might be a function of this particular test design, or of the particular groups of subjects. More experiments follow, all, we will suppose, impeccably designed, and the results seem to confirm the persistence of this accuracy order across a wide range of experimental conditions. So far, so good.

Accuracy and acquisition

But how do these results relate to the problem we began with? Do they show that learners follow a natural order in the internalization of the language system? The answer is: no, they do not. They provide evidence for an *accuracy* order in *performance*. Now we may wish to assume that an accuracy order is the same as an acquisitional order, but such an assumption is not warranted by the evidence, it is based on the speculation that language learners will reveal what they know, that their performance will be a reflection of their competence. But why should we suppose this to be the case? It may be that learners have internalized aspects of the system which for one reason or another they cannot access on particular occasions, that circumstances of different kinds prevent them from acting on this knowledge. This may seem a somewhat fanciful proposition, but no less a person than Chomsky has suggested such a possibility. He expresses it in the following way:

> Consider . . . a child learning English. Suppose that the child is at the stage at which he produces so-called 'telegraphic speech', that is, a series of content words without grammatical elements. Imagine the following (not entirely hypothetical) sequence of events. At one point the child produces only telegraphic speech. Shortly after, he makes correct use of grammatical particles such as 'do' and, let us say, the whole auxiliary system of English, and does so across the board, that is, in questions, assertions, negations, etc. At the earlier stage, the child did not have the capacity to use such items, so his behaviour indicates. Did he have the knowledge of the appropriate rules and forms? In the framework I am suggesting, the answer might be that he did. That is, it might be that he had fully internalized the requisite mental structure, but for some reason lacked the capacity to use it.   *(Chomsky 1980: 53)*

He goes on to add: '

> I see no reason to deny . . . that behaviour is only one kind of

evidence, sometimes not the best, and surely no criterion for knowledge.　*(Ibid: 54)*

Accuracy has to do with behaviour, acquisition has to do with knowledge. One cannot directly infer one from the other. The relationship between them is problematic. This point is elaborated in a recent paper (1985) by Bialystok and Sharwood-Smith (a development from Bialystok 1982). Here it is pointed out that there is a difference between knowledge of language and the ability to access that knowledge effectively in different contexts of use. Thus a learner may achieve a high accuracy profile in one context, which might suggest acquisition of certain forms, but perform badly on the same forms in a different context. This variation might either be because these forms are tied in some way to a particular kind of context and so are not freely transferable, or because the second context imposes inhibiting conditions which prevent learners from accessing and applying what they know. Either way, accuracy and acquisition do not match.

There is empirical evidence, too, against inferring acquired competence from relative accuracy of performance. Examples have been widely attested of learners who exhibit correct performance on certain forms, and then lapse into deviance later on. This may either be because of 'backsliding'—a reversion to a previous state of interlanguage—or it may be that the increased transferability of knowledge, which must to some degree involve analysis, calls for the recurrent dismantling and reassembling of linguistic forms which the learner may have internalized as complete formulaic units. Hence we might find instances of accuracy in the production of such formulas as fixed phrases but it does not follow that the learner can transfer the accurate production of forms to a wider range of constructions and contexts. Again, particular accuracy is not evidence for general acquisition (see Ellis 1985; Tarone 1983, 1988).

Now one would not wish to deny the value of extrapolation, of drawing general conclusions from the evidence of particular instances. But clearly we have to be careful to ensure that evidence for one phenomenon is not, either by accident or design, adduced in respect of another. The shift from evidence of accuracy in performance under certain conditions to general conclusions about internalization of competence is in principle no more justified than is the extrapolation from pigeon pecking to human verbal behaviour.

The Fundamental Pedagogical Principle

My reason for dwelling at some length on this matter of accuracy and acquisition is that the assumption that they are identical is a corner-stone to the whole edifice of a theory recently propounded which claims to provide a solution to the problems of language teaching which have plagued us for so long. I refer of course to the Monitor theory and its supposed corollaries. In a recent paper, Krashen, the sole begetter and main publicist of the Monitor theory, seeks to show how his theory leads to the postulation of 'The "Fundamental Pedagogical Principle" in second language teaching' (Krashen 1982, Krashen and Terrell 1983). *The* Fundamental Principle, proclaimed in capital letters with definite reference implying definitive solution. Is this what we have been waiting for all these years, the answer that has so far eluded us? Some teachers will believe so, particularly since it seems to be well founded on experimental findings. We should take a close look at what is being offered here before accepting it too readily.

Let us chart the way by which we arrive at the Fundamental Principle. Experimental studies have shown widespread consistency in accuracy orders by subjects of different kinds performing tasks requiring the production of certain linguistic forms. By a kind of rational conjuring, this is taken to mean that there is a natural order of *internalization* for these forms, a function in all probability of a universal Chomskyan Language Acquisition Device. Let us call this acquisition. All the empirical evidence in favour of accuracy order can now be shifted by sleight of hand in support of the notion of natural acquisition. That, briefly, is how the trick is done.

Acquisition and learning

But sometimes this natural acquisition order fails to make an appearance. On some tasks, subjects will perform with a degree of accuracy beyond what their state of acquisition should allow. How do we account for this? One might speculate, as I did myself several years ago (Widdowson 1979: Paper 15), that it is because the learner draws variably on his interim competence according to the situational demands made upon it; that his interlanguage, in other words, contains variable rules as well as invariant categorial ones and in this respect resembles fully fledged languages (see Ellis 1985, Chapter 4). Such a suggestion has at least the face validity of being consistent with the research done by Labov and others on language variation (see Hudson 1980: Chapter 5 for a review). But this is not the Krashen explanation for variable performance. Instead we have a different speculation: since learners do not always conform to the natural order (the argument goes), there must be an *un*natural order disrupting it. There must therefore be another process at work affecting performance, a process which is engaged for certain tasks but not for others. Let us call this *learning*, as distinct from *acquisition*. Learning is then a process of conscious intervention whereby performance initiated by the natural and unconscious process of acquisition is monitored, so that elements which have been learned as formal rules are grafted on to elements which emerge spontaneously from the domain of the unconscious. Two processes, then: acquisition, which is natural, unconscious, primary, and causative; and learning, which is unnatural, conscious, auxiliary, and corrective.

Now it follows by definition that learning can only be brought into operation when the occasion allows leisure for conscious thought about the language being used and its conformity to rule, when there is time to 'focus on form'. When learners are caught up in communication, concerned with making meaning, they have neither the time nor indeed the inclination to monitor their performance, which in consequence reveals what they have acquired without, as it were, the artificial additives of learning.

What empirical evidence is there that might persuade us to give credence to this sharp and absolute distinction? There are plenty of references to various studies which are pressed into support of this theory, giving it the appearance of authority. But on closer inspection it becomes clear that their validity as evidence depends crucially on how the key concepts in the theory are to be defined, and on what empirical conditions they have to meet to be sustained.

Consider, for example, two of the conditions which are said to be necessary for Monitor use: time and focus on form. We are told that 'in normal conversation, both in speaking and in listening, performers do not generally have time to think about and apply conscious grammatical rules' (Krashen 1981: 3). How do we know? Such an assertion presupposes a well-founded theory of performance, one which was able to assign periods of time to mental processes. The mind would appear to be fairly deft and rapid in its on-line operations: is it really incapable of referring to rules even when under conversational pressure? How long does it take to refer to a grammatical rule? Does it depend on the rule? Does it depend on who is doing the referring? Does it depend on what kind of conversation is in progress? I do not know the answers to any of these questions. But neither, I submit, does Krashen. And then, what does 'focus on form' mean? Is it not possible to focus on form because you want to make your meaning clear, because you want to be more communicatively effective? Why should focusing on form not be consistent with focusing on the message or on content, which is supposed to preclude the use of the monitor? The sharp dualism that is proposed whereby acquisition and learning are two quite distinct processes would seem to force the conclusion that if you think carefully, choose your words, take your time before making your conversational contribution you cannot communicate, or at any rate not very effectively, because you are interfering with the natural function of the acquired system. And since acquisition depends on communication, your deliberate delivery will impede your progress in learning the language as well.

In Krashen's theory, acquisition is the grand initiator of messages and the prime mover in communication. Communication, reflexively, creates conditions for the process of acquisition to take place. Learning plays a minor role in communicating and apparently is not itself affected by it. You cannot communicate with what you have learnt, nor it seems can you learn by communicating. But what is meant by communication? This, clearly, is another key concept in the theory, so how is it defined? The short answer is: it is not defined at all. But what indications we do have as to what is meant by communication are not very reassuring. We are told that the SLOPE test, for example, which yields results favourable to the natural order hypothesis, is communicative in character (Krashen 1981). It requires learners to provide a word to fill a blank in reference to a picture. For example:

Here is a ball.
Here are two . . . *(Picture)*
What is she doing here? *(Picture)*
She is . . . *(running, swimming, sitting down)*

To suggest that such a blank-filling exercise constitutes communicative behaviour is to generalize the concept so much as to make it almost meaningless. Does the whole conceptual perspective of the Monitor theory narrow down to a focus on filling in the blanks?

Communication and comprehensible input

But we have not yet arrived at the 'Fundamental Pedagogical Principle'. Acquisition is triggered by communicative activity. But this does not mean, apparently, the active negotiation of meaning, the realization of speech acts, discourse enactment, social interaction, or indeed any aspect of language use which those who have been concerned with communicative approaches to language teaching have found it necessary to invoke. There is no mention in the copious references attached to this theory of Austin or Searle, or Gumperz, Hymes or Labov, or of pragmatics, discourse analysis, ethnography or ethnomethodology. What communication reduces to is comprehensible input.

Exactly what is left out of account in this highly impoverished concept of communication is indicated by Richards and Schmidt in *Language and Communication* (1983). This is a collection of papers which makes extensive reference to the work I mention here. The beginning of the editors' introduction runs as follows:

> This book is intended for language teachers, teachers in training, and students of applied linguistics. The purpose of this book is to present a coherent survey of major issues in the study of language and communication, and to show how these are related to questions of practical concern in the learning and teaching of second and foreign languages. *(1983: xi)*

None of these major issues figures in Krashen's scheme of things, so he presumably does not regard them as having any relation at all to the learning and teaching of languages.

Morrison and Low, in one of the papers in *Language and Communication*, refer directly to the distortions brought about by the narrowness of Krashen's perspective. In particular, they point out that the phenomenon of monitoring cannot be confined within the restricted role it plays in Monitor theory:

> While the monitoring function is clearly an interesting and important aspect of language learning and language use, one

feels it deserves to be represented as a complex and subtle activity, responsive to a variety of social and psychological pressures. *(1983:231)*

The authors argue that monitoring, properly understood, is a crucial feature of communicative interaction. Monitoring, as understood by Krashen, would appear to play no positive part in communication whatever.

One sees once more how a failure in the proper *conceptualization* of the issues to be investigated can compromise an enquiry, no matter how much empirical evidence is on display. The narrowness of vision that Morrison and Low pinpoint is actually not unlike that of Skinner (referred to earlier in this chapter), which Chomsky attacked to such deadly effect. Monitor theory and reinforcement theory would seem to have a good deal in common.

So it is the provision of comprehensible input which is the 'Fundamental Pedagogical Principle'. Learners acquire a particular language by receiving comprehensible input, that is to say by being exposed to messages expressed in language which is within the current acquired competence of the learners, together with language which is due to appear in the next stage of acquisition, and which can be eased into the mind by the help of context, knowledge of the world and so on.

The solution to our problems as teachers, then, is to provide comprehensible input. It does not appear to matter whether the learners are particularly interested in this input, or what they actually do with it, or whether they are actively engaged in achieving purposeful outcomes. They do, it is true, have to lower their affective filter to allow the input to flow in, but this might be achieved in all manner of ways. The theory only requires that the learner should be a kind of humanoid receptacle in a maximal state of receptivity so that the input can enter to work its mysterious way.

In recent Second Language Acquisition (SLA) research (for example, Long 1983a) there has been a recognition that the learner does not naturally assume the role of passive recipient but is actively involved in the process of manipulating the input so that it is optimally comprehensible. Long points out that in native speaker/non-native speaker (NS/NNS) interactions, both participants collaborate in recipient design by employing strategies for negotiating meaning. In this respect, the learner exercises his own initiative to ensure the proper supply of comprehensible input.

But the question then arises as to whether all this interactive effort serves only to facilitate the internalization of linguistic knowledge, as Long appears to imply, or whether it does not also develop the executive ability referred to earlier, whereby the learner can access that knowledge in a range of communicative contexts. The emergence of this question (which I shall return to in subsequent chapters) shows how an enquiry which seeks to provide a solution to one problem generates issues which, if taken up, can lead to a reconsideration of the problem. In this case, instead of accepting that comprehensible input is indeed validly conceived as 'The "Fundamental Pedagogical Principle"' and then looking at how it might be achieved by interaction, one might more profitably ask whether these strategies of interaction on the part of the learner do not suggest that the notion of comprehensible input is inadequate for explaining how language is learned, and therefore is not so very fundamental after all.

The reduction of the concept of communication to comprehensible input, in association with the absence of any clear definition of what is meant by comprehensible or any criteria for knowing whether language has been comprehended or not, means that almost any approach to teaching can claim to have the blessing of the theory. Direct Method, for example, provides an abundance of comprehensible input: *Hand. This is my hand. Ear. This is my ear. This is my ear. Two ears. I have two ears.* So does direct translation. After all, the presence of the first language is likely to allay anxiety, increase the sense of security and generally dispose learners to lower their affective filter. At the same time, of course, it assures them of comprehensible input. These methods are, in the terms of the theory, communicative approaches to language teaching. All the problems that we have been wrestling with over recent years in attempting to formulate a set of principles for communicative language teaching suddenly vanish as if at the waving of a wand. All our efforts are rendered irrelevant.

At this point I want to make it quite clear that I have discussed Monitor theory in some detail not to criticize it as such (cf. McLaughlin 1978, 1987; Gregg 1984; White 1987), but what it represents. In fact, I find the ideas of considerable interest, being myself naturally disposed to speculation. But my purpose in dwelling on this theory is to demonstrate how ideas are spread by the action of persuasion on uncritical acquiescence and get converted into solutions, which are assumed to be valid everywhere, like American Express traveller's cheques. Monitor theory is not, of course, the only theory which has laid claim to such universal solving powers. Behaviourism, with its reduction of language learning to habit formation, is another example. There are indeed, as I have already suggested, certain similarities between the two theories, and they have similar powers of deception and similar capacities for making mischief.

The relativity and relevance of research

The essential point is that there are no universal solutions. We should not expect that research will come up with recipes and remedies which will work whatever the circumstances. We should recognize that the validity of research findings is always *relative*, and relative in two quite different ways. First, it is relative to the conditions which are imposed on a particular empirical enquiry. It does not follow that if subjects are induced to behave in a certain way within the idealized limits of experimental control, they will behave in the same way when these limits are relaxed. In a sense, experimental subjects are only partially real people. We come back here, of course, to the question of extrapolation which I mentioned earlier.

The first kind of relativity, then, has to do with the conditions that define the methodology of enquiry. The second kind has to do with the conceptual coherence of the theory that the empirical investigation is designed to support. If, for example, we have no clear definition of what exactly is meant by communication or comprehensible input, how can we recognize what is evidence and what is not? If we are not provided with a reasoned argument in its support, why should we accept, as if it were self-evident, that accuracy and acquisition orders are the same? No matter how rigorously designed empirical studies may be, their value is always relative to the explicit formulation of the theory they are designed to serve. Excellent technology will not compensate for poor science. The value of empirical research ultimately depends on the quality of conceptual analysis that defines the objects of enquiry.

But if research is so unreliable as a source of solutions, what good is it? In my view, the value of research is that it can help teachers to define more clearly the problems that they themselves must solve. What it can do is to stimulate interest and encourage teachers to think about the implications of their practices. It can also provide them with a conceptual context within which to work, in the form of hypotheses to test out in the conditions of their particular classrooms. In short, theory can help practitioners to adopt a theoretical orientation to their task, whereby they seek to refer the particular techniques they use to more general principles, and, reciprocally, test out the validity of such principles against the observed actualities of classroom practice.

Some years ago, Evelyn Hatch gave characteristically wise counsel to teachers about applying research findings to classroom teaching: *apply with caution* (Hatch 1979). I would go further and say: *do not apply at all*. We cannot exercise caution unless we know how to interpret such findings in terms of actual conditions, other than those which define the relative validity of these findings. This suggests that it is not the findings, the *products* of enquiry, that we should apply but the *process* of enquiry, the conceptual analysis, observation and experimentation which research exemplifies. Simply to apply findings, without regard to their particular conditions of validity, is to impose prescribed patterns of behaviour on learners as if they were subjects rather than people and to make them submit to solutions which correspond to problems other than their own. To adopt such a pedagogy is to follow the example of Procrustes who, it will be recalled, would either stretch his guests on a rack or cut pieces off their lower limbs so that they would fit his bed.

The *pedagogic* relevance of research outside the classroom can only be realized by research inside the classroom. This is not to diminish the importance of controlled empirical study and the value of its findings, but to suggest that the extent of its usefulness can only be established by continuing enquiry and experimentation in the classroom. This too is research, even though we may not honour it with the name. I think it is convenient, and not too misleading, to conceive of research outside the classroom, both of the soft speculative and the hard empirical varieties, as resulting in kinds of stereotypes. As with the stereotypes we refer to in the business of everyday life, we know they are not, and cannot be, comprehensively true or correct, but they provide us with an indispensable framework within which we can interpret particular instances. They are frameworks for assessment, not formulas to be rigidly applied. And if people and pupils do not fit the stereotypic formula, we will, I hope, be disinclined to maim them into conformity, but to adjust the dimensions of the bed to accommodate them.

Over the past ten years or so there has been a great deal of innovative thinking and impressive empirical investigation in our field and the theory I have been reviewing has played its part. All this enquiry has led not to the definitive 'Fundamental Pedagogical Principle', but to a quite fundamental reappraisal of pedagogic principles in general. That is to say, it has indicated ways of redefining our problems. But it is idle, and indeed pernicious, to suppose that it has provided solutions of any worthwhile generality. We cannot expect that the experience and experiments of other people in other places occupied with other problems will produce answers off the peg which will fit our particular requirements.

This is just as well, otherwise the practice of language teaching would have no claim to any professional status, for such a claim is not consistent with a reliance on ready-made solutions. It rests on a readiness on the part of practitioners to pursue their own enquiries in the very process of classroom teaching. How such enquiries might be conducted is a question which is considered in the next chapter.

3 The pragmatics of language teaching

The question of relevance

How should language teachers react to the besetting influence of ideas about language and learning which emerge from the domains of disciplinary enquiry, from research in linguistics, psychology, sociology, philosophy, and education? They can, of course, declare their independence, refuse, so to speak, to be beset, and carry on as if these ideas were not there. This does not seem to me a very sensible strategy, because on the face of it these ideas would appear to be of potential relevance to pedagogic practice. The question is, how is this potential to be realized? How is relevance to be determined? Different domains of enquiry and action work to different criteria of significance. There is no reason to suppose that what goes on in one domain is necessarily relevant to what goes on in another. Relevance is a matter of significance to one's own concerns. But the concerns of pedagogy are the business of teachers. It is surely they who have to determine relevance in this case, they who have to be convinced that what research has to say has a bearing on what they do. In other words, it is they who have to act as mediators between theory and practice, between the domains of disciplinary research and pedagogy.

How is the mediating role of teachers to be defined and how can they be guided to adopt it? Equally, how is language pedagogy to be defined in relation to other areas of enquiry that impinge upon it? Unless these issues are satisfactorily resolved, ideas emerging from disciplinary study cannot be effectively assessed or acted upon in the pedagogic domain.

This chapter seeks to set up a scheme for language teacher education, a pragmatics of pedagogy, which incorporates these conditions for establishing relevance and provides for the furtherance of proper and profitable relations between theory and practice.

The pragmatics of language pedagogy

By the pragmatics of pedagogy, I mean the working out of a reflexive, interdependent relationship between theory and practice, between abstract ideas deriving from various areas of enquiry and their actualization in the achievement of practical outcomes. The realization of this relationship in the act of teaching (which I maintain is the only way it can be effectively realized) has reciprocal effects. On the one hand it provides for the possibility of improved techniques for bringing about learning; on the other it provides a rationale whereby such techniques can be explicitly identified as exemplars of more general principles of teaching. Seen in this way, the reflexive nature of pragmatism, with theory realized in practice, practice informed by theory, brings mutual benefits in that it serves the cause both of effective learning and, as a corollary, of the professional development of the teacher.

As I indicated in the preceding chapter, innovative approaches to language teaching that have been recommended in the past have not, generally speaking, been subjected to this kind of pragmatic treatment. Such recommendations have a non-reflexive and unilateral character: they derive from theory and determine practice. Typically, the teacher is called upon to implement the second order realization of new ideas in the form of teaching materials rather than to consider the ideas themselves and how they key in with his own experience of teaching. Teaching materials usually provide very little in the way of explicit rationale which would enable teachers to modify them in a principled way with reference to the ideas which inform them. They are designed not for experimentation but for implementation. The teacher acts as medium.

But pragmatism, as I am using the term here, is a function of pedagogic *mediation* whereby the relationship between theory and practice, ideas and their actualization, can only be realized within the domain of application, that is, through the immediate activity of teaching. In this view, teaching materials are to be seen as hypothetical constructs, models or exemplars of abstract principles from which actual instances of pedagogic activities might be developed in the light of particular classroom conditions. They have the same ideal character as does any abstract model of reality and its canonical exemplification, and their relationship with actual states of affairs is a matter of continual interpretation and reappraisal.

The dangers of disregarding, by ignorance or design, the essentially *conditional* nature of abstract models and of making data fit into preconceived categories are well attested in the theoretical domain. The dangers are no less apparent in the practical domain: they are attested in countless classrooms where teaching is confined to the transmission of textbook material rather than its exploitation for the negotiation of appropriate activities for learning. The relationship between linguistic theory, the description of a particular language based upon it, and the way that language is actualized as behaviour in contexts of use is analagous to the relationship between a pedagogic theory of language learning, the devising of teaching materials based upon it, and the way that language is most effectively actualized for learning in the contexts of particular classrooms. The relationship is a pragmatic one in both cases: the connection between the ideal and the real needs to be established by mediation.

A model of mediation

With regard to pedagogic mediation (teaching as a pragmatic activity) two interdependent processes seem to be involved. The first of these we might refer to as *appraisal*. This focuses on theory and consists of the *interpretation* of ideas within their own terms of reference, within the context of their own theoretical provenance, and the *evaluation* of their relevance or validity in principle with reference to the domain of enquiry which constitutes the context of application. Evaluation, then, is the process of specifying what might be called the transfer value of ideas.

The second pragmatic process might be called *application*. This connects with practice and also can be conceived of as a two-stage operation. First, ideas are actually put into *operation* in the practical domain and then the consequences are monitored in a second process of *evaluation*, this time directed at establishing the practical effect of the ideas as operationally realized.

Appraisal, then, is a conceptual evaluation based on a proper understanding of the ideas proposed, and it is directed at establishing a set of valid principles of general relevance. Application is an empirical evaluation based on teaching experience and has to do with the devising of effective techniques specific to particular circumstances. Application can, of course, lead to reappraisal, just as empirical evidence in other areas of research can lead to a reformulation or abandonment of initial hypotheses. There is, however, always the problem of knowing whether the fault in the mediation process lies in the validity of the principle or in the particular techniques that have been used to operationalize it. This problem is very much in evidence in language teaching too. It is a problem that can never be finally resolved. And it is the impossibility of ultimate resolution that makes pedagogic mediation a continuous process of enquiry and experiment. If this process is arrested and teaching reduced to the manipulation of a set of techniques, or conformity to a fixed method, then pedagogy as such ceases to exist.

We might make a diagram of the mediation process in the following way:

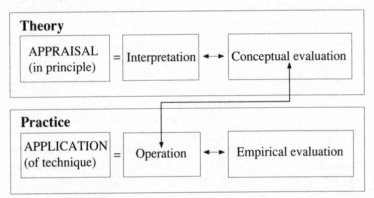

Figure 1

Applied linguists and language teachers

It is, I think, commonly supposed that there is a division of responsibility in respect to these two main aspects of mediation. Appraisal is seen to be principally the activity of applied linguistics (or that branch of it that concerns itself with language teaching) and application (as defined here) the principal activity of language teaching. In some respects, this is a reasonable supposition to make. The roles of applied linguist and language teacher are different; they work to different professional briefs. The former does not have a full-time commitment to the classroom and so has no occasion to engage in operational activities and empirical evaluation as intrinsic to the pedagogic process. The latter, fully engaged in this process, has little opportunity to go in pursuit of relevant insights from the informing disciplines. If one is to recognize that there are applied linguists and language teachers in the world identifiable by the difference of role they play (even though these roles may exist in different degrees of convergence) then the division of responsibility which corresponds with appraisal and application seems to be just about the only one to make. But it is the *relationship* between these roles, as between the two aspects of mediation, which is crucial.

I have argued that it is the teachers' task to mediate through everyday pedagogic activity: it is their exercise of pragmatism which should achieve the double objective of learning outcome and professional development. It follows that it is the applied linguists' task to facilitate mediation since their role precludes any direct engagement with this process on their own account. Their contribution is to identify ideas of likely relevance and to present argument and evidence for validity in an accessible way. Their business is to propound ideas in such a way that their claimed transfer value is made explicit for the consideration and possible operationalization by the teacher. Of course, the propounding may be very persuasive and the teacher needs to be wary. But the teachers are in charge in the scheme of things proposed here. The applied linguists have the subordinate and supporting role. What they have to say by way of appraisal has no effective force unless it is incorporated into the mediation process enacted by teachers and under thier control.

The relationship between applied linguistics and language pedagogy is explored in a collection of papers presented at the Georgetown Round Table on Languages and Linguistics in 1983 (Alatis, Stern, and Strevens 1983). It is of interest to compare the positions of Brumfit and Krashen in this collection, positions which might be said to typify to some degree the attitudes to applied linguistics and language teaching on each side of the Atlantic.

For Brumfit, applied linguistics is seen as accountable to pedagogy in the sense that it is the teacher who is the ultimate arbiter of relevance. The starting point of theory is in the problems of classroom practice: the researcher's domain is that of the teacher.

They [i.e. researchers] must be concerned with providing a

model of interpretation of evidence from theory and experiment, related to the solution of the practical problems which immediately present themselves to classroom teachers. They will be demonstrating, in other words, the continuing process of adaptation and adjustment without which, as we well know from observation, teaching can easily stagnate into a set of half-understood routines, performed irrespective of the conditions of the class or the needs of the learners. *(Brumfit in Alatis, Stern, and Strevens 1983: 62)*

Krashen too sees the value of theory as providing for adaptation:

If we provide teachers with only one method, we are doing them a disservice. The teacher will be unprepared for change and will not have the flexibility needed to adapt to new situations . . . When we provide theory, we provide them with the underlying rationale for methodology in general. This permits adaptation for different situations, evaluations of new techniques and evaluation of materials. *(Krashen in Alatis, Stern, and Strevens 1983: 261)*

Thus far, Krashen's position would seem to correspond closely with that of Brumfit, and indeed to the pragmatic rationale which I am proposing here. But it becomes clear that Krashen is not thinking of *theory in general*, that is to say of a theoretical perspective on pedagogy, but of *a theory in particular* which can be applied directly; not, therefore, of the process of referring actual problems to abstract ideas but the process of making practice conform to a preconceived conceptual pattern. He is seeking to impose a method. There is no pragmatic reciprocity here. He goes on:

The theory must be *a* theory of second language acquisition, not a theory of grammatical structure, and *it must be consistent with all known research*, not merely armchair speculation. *(Ibid: 1983: 261 [my italics])*

The theory which Krashen has in mind is of course his own. As I have indicated in the preceding chapter, this theory is not in fact consistent with all known research (it is doubtful if *any* theory could be that) nor is it free of speculation.

But the important point to note is that the adherence to *a* theory which Krashen proposes actually precludes the exercise of pragmatic options and the quest for relevance which characterize a theoretical orientation to pedagogy of the kind outlined in this chapter. In other words it does not use theory to activate the crucial process of mediation.

Mediation failure

Mediation can of course fail (and has failed in the past) at different phases in the process. There can be evaluation of validity, positive or negative, without the proper interpretation of ideas. This can lead to fervent acceptance or rejection uninformed by understanding, the imposition of one mode of thinking on another. All this raises the whole issue of the relationship between interpretation and conceptual evaluation which I touched on in Chapter 2. A failure to recognize that interpretation and conceptual evaluation are different may lead to the assumption that ideas from one area of enquiry are self-evidently relevant to another. It has been assumed, for example, that the units of language analysis that figure in models of linguistic description are necessarily valid as units of language for pedagogic purposes. The central issue here is the relationship between the *description* of language and the *prescription* of language for pedagogic purposes. The shift over recent years to the data-based study of actually occurring language, as distinct from a reliance on the linguist's intuition as a representative user, has yielded new information about English—for example, new facts about frequency of usage and about the use of language in the achievement of meaning in context. A number of scholars have shown that these facts are left unaccounted for in standard descriptions of the language and in the prescriptions which are provided in syllabuses (Coates 1982; Labov 1984; Sinclair 1985; Stubbs 1986a). This is what Sinclair has to say:

> I think that we are on the verge of a major reorientation in language description—one that will create problems for anyone who thinks that the facts are known. I am compelled to take this view by the early results of computer processing of language text. The picture is quite disturbing. On the one hand, there is now ample evidence of the existence of significant language patterns which have gone largely un-recorded in centuries of study; on the other hand there is a dearth of support for some phenomena which are regularly

put forward as normal patterns of English.   *(Sinclair 1985: 251)*

It should be noted, however, that the relationship between descriptive fact and pedagogic prescription cannot be one of determinacy. Before the advent of the computer, H. E. Palmer, Michael West and others carried out word frequency studies on a corpus of language data with a view to determining the content of language courses. They discovered that compromises had to be made between the descriptive criteria of frequency and range of language items and pedagogic criteria which were adduced from the assumed purpose or process of learning (see Mackey 1965: Chapter 6; Widdowson 1968: Chapter 1). One such pedagogic criterion is coverage:

> The coverage or covering capacity of an item is the number of things one can say with it. It can be measured by the number of other items which it can displace.   *(Mackey 1965: 184)*

The criterion of coverage is likely to prevail over frequency in cases where the *purpose* of learning is to acquire a minimal productive competence across a limited range of predictable situations.

There is a *process* version of this criterion which we might call valency. By this I mean the potential of an item to generate further learning. Thus we might wish to teach a particular structure or word meaning not on the grounds of frequency of occurrence but because its acquisition provides a basis for the learner to understand and learn other structures or meanings by extension. The item which is most used is not necessarily the item which is most useful for learning.

Consider an example from the new Collins Cobuild dictionary (1987), of which Sinclair is editor-in-chief and which is based on just the kind of computer analysis of text that he refers to. With respect to the lexical item *bet*, analysis reveals the descriptive fact that what we might call the canonical meaning of the word, 'to lay a wager', is relatively rarely attested as compared with its very frequent informal occurrence as a modal marker indicating conviction as in expressions like 'I bet he'll turn up tomorrow', 'There's no milk in the fridge, I bet'. As Sinclair points out in his introduction (p. xix), this fact about frequency does not determine the order of appearance of dictionary entries: there is the factor of the native speakers' sense of what is the core meaning, for example. Nor does it follow that this second meaning should be given *pedagogic* preference over the first. Here too there are reasons for reversing the priority.

In the first place, the informal modal meaning tends to be restricted to the grammatical environment of first person singular and present tense and in this respect to have limited productive generality. It takes on something of the character of an idiom. With other persons and tenses, the word assumes its other more fully lexical meaning as in:

I bet her he would turn up yesterday.
He'll bet there's no milk in the fridge.

Or the result is an ungrammatical expression, as in:

*There's no milk in the fridge, he bets.

There are good pedagogic reasons for avoiding idiomatic idiosyncrasy of this kind.

In the second place, the modal meaning is derivable from the canonical lexical meaning but not the other way round. Thus if the learner knows that *bet* means 'to lay a wager', it is possible to infer the modal sense by extension when it is encountered in use. It is in this sense that the former has a greater valency and so constitutes a better learning investment. We might indeed propose a general principle: high valency items are to be taught so that high frequency items can be more effectively learned.

Techniques for the analysis of textual data have become very sophisticated and these lead to descriptive refinements beyond the scope of Palmer and West. But the relationship between description and prescription has still to be worked out: the principle of pedagogic accountability remains in force. This matter will come up again in later parts of the book. At present what we need to note is the recognition of the validity of a description in its own terms does not commit us to acknowledge its pedagogic relevance in principle. It still needs to be evaluated in other terms to be effectively mediated into practice.

Again, mediation failure may occur when ideas are put into operation in the application phase without being subjected to adequate appraisal. This is what happens in the cases of textbook transmission that I referred to earlier: the teacher is required only to put into operation ideas which have already been realized as materials and is given no guidance in the evaluation of the validity of the principles on which the materials have been designed even when these principles are clear to the textbook writers themselves.

A number of implications arise from the model of pragmatic mediation that I have sketched out here. First, the process, as outlined in the diagram, is a scheme for research as well as for teaching conventionally considered: each is seen as a concomitant of the other, and it is this which provides for the professional development of the teacher. The question then arises as to how this pragmatic enterprise differs, if it differs at all, from the kinds of activity which are customarily carried out under the name of research. Related to this question of pedagogic/pragmatic research as an integrated element of classroom practice is the matter of teacher formation. What kind of preparation or priming do teachers need in order to exploit their classroom experience in the manner I have suggested? The concepts of education and training in the professional development of teachers are relevant here. These implications are explored in some detail in the next chapter, but in this one I want to elaborate a little on the model itself by considering more closely how it bears upon certain current issues in the pedagogy of language teaching.

Issues in appraisal and application

1   *Interpretation*

Interpretation must always be a matter of matching up what is new to what is familiar: ideas can only be understood in reference to established categories of thought. There is always the tendency, therefore, to adjust ideas so that they conform to what is conventional and customary. Yet conventional categories can be modified also to allow for change in concepts and attitudes. We have, then, two opposing processes at work whose tensions create the dialectical conditions for gradual change. They can be seen as large-scale social variants of Piaget's psychological processes of assimilation and accommodation (see, for example, Piaget 1955). New ideas may be assimilated into given modes of thinking or given modes of thinking may be altered to accommodate new ideas.

Generally speaking, it has been assimilation rather than accommodation which has characterized interpretation in the domain of language pedagogy over recent years. This has had two effects. On the one hand, ideas have been simplified into reduced versions which often bear little resemblance to their originals in the disciplinary contexts from which they have been taken. On the other hand, the potential of these ideas for the development of new lines of thought in pedagogy has been under-exploited.

Take, for example, the idea of 'communicative competence'. This is a complex and still unstable concept whose understanding involves a consideration of a range of issues within discourse analysis, pragmatics, and the theory of grammar (see, for example, Canale and Swain 1980; Richards and Schmidt 1983). Yet the idea is frequently interpreted to mean simply the ability to produce spoken utterances which are marked for illocutionary function: promising, warning, recommending, agreeing, predicting, and so on. And a syllabus which defines its content in functional terms is supposed to account for communicative competence in a way which syllabuses designed on other principles cannot.

Consider the following remarks:

> The advantage of the notional syllabus is that it takes the communicative facts of language into account from the beginning without losing sight of grammatical and situational factors. It is potentially superior to the grammatical syllabus because it will produce a communicative competence. *(Wilkins 1976: 19)*

I would argue that no syllabus, however conceived and designed, can *produce* a communicative competence. A syllabus is simply an inert specification. Only when it is actualized through classroom activity can it have an effect on learning. The syllabus is a scheme for teachers and its influence on learners is only indirect, mediated by methodology.

Whether or not a notional syllabus will help to *promote* a communicative competence will depend on just how it is used, how grammatical and situational factors are taken into account in the manner of its implementation. Wilkins' proposals, for example, have been widely taken to sanction the teaching of more or less fixed phrases as standard expressions of function (requesting, inviting, describing, agreeing, disagreeing, etc.). But the ability to produce such phrases does not constitute communicative competence in so far as I understand the concept

(Widdowson 1978, 1979, 1983, 1984a, 1989), or as discussed in, for example, Canale and Swain 1980, and Bachman 1990.

Proposals for syllabuses based on this reduced notion of communication also illustrate how the potential for change inherent in new ideas is stifled by assimilation into established patterns of thinking. The syllabus is still conceived of as a collection of atomistic linguistic elements even though they are now functionally rather than formally defined. It is still regarded as a preconceived construct which incorporates *goals* for learning, and its relationship with a methodology which activates the immediate *process* of learning remains as undefined as before.

But the idea of communicative competence arises from a dissatisfaction with the Chomskyan distinction between competence and performance and essentially seeks to establish competence status for aspects of language behaviour which were indiscriminately collected into the performance category. Now it seems reasonable to suggest that the competence/performance distinction might also mark the division of responsibility between syllabus and methodology, with the former specifying the knowledge to be acquired and the latter providing conditions for its behavioural realization. One might have expected, therefore, that this issue about the nature and scope of linguistic description would have been interpreted as a derived issue, so to speak, in respect of syllabus design and methodology. There is little sign that this has happened. Over recent years there has been a growing realization that the development of communicative competence is crucially a methodological matter, but we also need a rationale in support of such a shift of focus. Similarly there is a recognition that grammar has an importance in language learning which a too enthusiastic pursuit of functions has tended to ignore, and grammar reference books and exercises of all kinds (and all qualities) are now springing out of publishing houses. But a proper understanding of the concept of communicative competence would have revealed that it gives no endorsement for the neglect of grammar. And now that grammar is coming back into favour, there does not seem to be much in the way of reasoned argument for its return. It was left out before, it is put back now. Why? Many seem to be content to say that fashions change and that's that. This is hardly an attitude which is conducive to a principled development of pedagogic thinking.

One might say that in the light of the passage quoted on page 39 there is no endorsement for the neglect of grammar in Wilkins' proposals either. The notional syllabus, as he describes it, does take grammatical factors into account (or at least, does not lose sight of them). However, it should be noted that *any* method of presenting language will take grammatical factors into account contingently in the sense that any linguistic expression will of its very nature manifest grammatical categories. The issue is not whether such factors will in some way be represented, because they are bound to be, but whether they are in pedagogic focus. The central question is how far and in what ways does a syllabus encourage the teacher to direct learners to an explicit awareness of grammatical factors. Much of the work that claims to follow a notional/functional line of approach leaves grammar as an implied presence: in sight, perhaps, but not in mind. Whether this is a failure in the interpretation of the evaluation of Wilkins' ideas is an open question.

I shall discuss the role of grammar as a necessary communicative resource in later chapters of this book. For now, the point I wish to make is that in regard to the notional/functional syllabus, although there is a change in the way of describing the content units for language teaching, this change tends to be assimilated into traditional and well-established ways of thinking about the syllabus as a pedagogic construct. The fillers change but they are assimilated into slots which remain the same. So notions and functions are generally seen as *replacing* linguistic structures as units of content, and a notional/functional (and therefore communicative) orientation is seen to be incompatible with a concern for grammatical structure and meanings intrinsic in form. There is little room for accommodation.

This is particularly paradoxical and revealing in the case of notions. To begin with, the term *notion* is itself a cause of some confusion since it has been interpreted in different ways in relation to its companion *function*. Wilkins himself consistently uses the term notion to refer to both kinds of category he talks about, semantic and pragmatic: the term *notion* incorporates functions. Conversely, Halliday uses the term *function* to refer to the formal encoding of meaning within a grammar (see, for example, Halliday 1985). In this semantico-grammatical sense the term *function* incorporates notions. Let us clarify matters by using the term *notion* to refer to what Wilkins calls semantico-grammatical categories, and *function* to refer uniquely to what

Wilkins calls categories of communicative function. This would seem to accord quite closely with common usage.

Now notions in this sense have, of course, always been accounted for in conventional syllabus design. The lexical items and the formal patterns they fill, which constitute the content units of a structural syllabus, are precisely semantico-grammatical categories. They are *formal* in character and have to do with language at the level of the sentence and its constituents. The notional/functional syllabus offers nothing of novelty here. What *is* novel in notional/functional proposals is the comprehensive inclusion, within syllabus specification, of what Wilkins calls 'categories of communicative function'. These have to do not with formal but with *pragmatic* meaning. They cannot be fixed in advance but are conditional on context because they relate not to sentences but to utterances. The crucial question that arises here, therefore, is how the given categories of grammar which constitute the content units of a structural syllabus are to be associated with the new categories of communicative function: in other words, how (to use Halliday's terms this time) the meaning potential intrinsic in language form gets realized in the pragmatic achievement of meaning.

The very raising of such a question makes it evident that notional/functional syllabus proposals actually imply an *extension* of previous practices, a development from the structural approach to syllabus design with the semantico-grammatical notions as the essential transition, common to both. But in fact the notional/functional approach has generally been represented as a radical departure, a complete break with the past. In consequence, that aspect of it which links it with previous practice has diminished almost at times to the point of disappearance. Functions tend to dominate the scene with notions appearing in a separate sub-plot in a relatively minor role. As to the functions themselves, they are deprived of their pragmatic identity and cast in a role in which they resemble the grammatical units that they replace.

So we see ideas about the nature of communication interpreted in a reductive way, assimilated into preconceived ways of thinking to make them amenable to conventional pedagogic treatment. They are not examined with a view to appraisal which might require adjustments to concepts of syllabus design to accommodate them.

In fact, a close consideration of work done in discourse

processing would raise the possibility of even more radical accommodation. For example, there is evidence to suggest that a good deal of communication is achieved not so much by the on-line assembly of analysed items but by the adaptation of formuliac phrases (see, for example, Pawley and Syder 1983). It would appear that such procedures, whereby pre-existing patterns are adjusted by differential focusing, are a feature of first language learning (see, for example, Peters 1983). So it would seem reasonable to suggest that second language learners might proceed in a similar way (cf. Hakuta 1974). This would provide some explanation for the phenomenon of variation in interlanguage systems (see Tarone 1983; Ellis 1985).

If one follows through the possible implications of this, one comes to the thought that perhaps language should be presented to learners primarily in lexical terms, setting conditions for the gradual emergence of syntax as a focusing device—the very converse of conventional practice.

This conception of syntax as a kind of lexical auxiliary is explored in Chapter 5. I mention it here simply to illustrate the implications that might arise from the more considered inter-pretation of theoretical ideas. There are of course cases where the implications of ideas about communication have been thought through and subjected to more accommodating inter-pretation. It would be wrong to suggest otherwise. But this kind of critical thinking needs to be encouraged and sustained throughout the language teaching profession as a whole, as, indeed, a necessary condition on its professionalism. Otherwise ideas which should instigate appraisal will continue to be made into simple tokens for easy assimilation, converted into catch-phrases or vague, fashionable buzz-words in vogue, and instead of rational development, we shall continue to get change which comes only with the vagaries of fashion.

All interpretation requires the reconciliation of the competing claims of assimilation and accommodation. Too much accom-modation and one loses one's bearings in the necessary con-ventions of thought. Too much assimilation and one is becalmed in the doldrums and no progress is possible at all. The problem is to know how to strike the right balance. What is needed as far as language teachers are concerned is some way of making them aware of the problem as it relates to their professional work and of providing the means whereby they might arrive at interpreta-tions appropriate to themselves.

I have talked about interpretation which is accommodating so that it yields implications for language teaching. But not all implications are valid in reference to pedagogy. One can accept that a certain theoretical position or set of research findings leads to certain conclusions, but one can still question whether these conclusions are relevant to one's own case. The dividing line here is a tenuous one if it exists at all. It is probably a matter of degree of accommodation: the more you accommodate an idea the more committed you become to an acceptance of its validity. Accommodating interpretation implies a degree of evaluation, which for the purposes of this chapter I would like to consider separately.

2   Conceptual evaluation

There are two general assumptions which seem to be widely if not universally accepted as self-evident. They are (to give them convenient labels) the means/end equation, and the efficiency of natural learning. I do not think that in either case there has been any failure in interpretation of the ideas proposed, but rather that accommodation has been too readily accorded. In short I believe the assumptions to be consistent with proposed ideas, but of doubtful validity when subjected to evaluation.

The means/ends equation and the concept of authenticity. By the means/ends equation, I mean the assumption that what the learner has eventually to achieve by way of language ability should determine what he does in the process of acquiring that ability. Thus if learners are aiming to communicate naturally, they need to be prepared for this by being involved in natural communicative language use in the classroom. In short, the language of the classroom has to be authentic. The belief here is that the language behaviour of natural use, which is the end of learning, should be replicated as closely as possible in the classroom as this language behaviour will also be conductive to learning, to the means whereby communicative ability is achieved.

I have argued against this position elsewhere (Widdowson 1979, 1984a). This is not to say that the position is wrong but only that it is arguable, or in other words, open to conceptual evaluation.

Authenticity of language in the classroom is bound to be, to some extent, an illusion. This is because it does not depend on the source from which the language as an object is drawn but on the learners' engagement with it. In actual language use, as the work on discourse analysis and pragmatics makes abundantly clear, meanings are achieved by human agency and are negotiable: they are not contained in text. To the extent that language learners, by definition, are deficient in competence they cannot authenticate the language they deal with in the manner of the native speaker. The language presented to them may be a genuine record of native speaker behaviour, genuine, that is to say, as textual data, but to the extent that it does not engage native speaker response it cannot be realized as authentic discourse.

Furthermore, if authenticity is to be defined as natural language behaviour (and it is hard to see how else it might be defined) there is also the difficulty that learners will naturally incline to draw on their own language in any situation that calls for uncontrived linguistic communication. So the situations which are to stimulate the use of the language being learned will have to be contrived in some way, and the learners will have to co-operate in maintaining the illusion of reality. They will have to be a party to the pretence and accept that the activities in class are, to use a Goffman term, 'framed' as classroom events (Goffman 1974).

Even when increased authenticity might be judged to be desirable on motivational grounds, one is faced with the problem that the process of learning depends on the recognition of underlying regularities, on the identification of salient and essential features from all the accidental complexities of actual behaviour. It may be generally true that the natural language use which constitutes the goal of learning is realized by a focus on meaning rather than form, and is a matter of top-down rather than bottom-up processing, but the process of arriving at that goal, the development of the authenticating ability, calls for an effective internalization of form and capability of analysis which will allow for their use across a wide and unpredictable range of different contexts. In other words, the very learning process implies a focus on form as a necessary condition for the subsequent focus on meaning.

The idea that learners should be discouraged from attending to the formal properties of language is comparable to the idea, prevalent in a previous era, that learners should be denied all access to translation. Learners will attend to form and make use of translation anyway because the learning process requires them to do so. A pedagogy which denies this perversely creates difficulties which hamper the learner in this task. The central question is not what learners have to do to use language naturally, but what they have to do to *learn* to use language naturally. In my view the authenticity argument is invalid because it does not distinguish between the two questions: it confuses ends and means and assumes that teaching language *for* communication is the same as teaching language *as* communication (cf. Widdowson 1984a: Paper 16). But no doubt these conclusions too are open to challenge. This is why the issue needs to be evaluated for its pedagogic validity to be established.

One way of proceeding would be to distinguish different senses of the term *authenticity*. This is what Breen does. He suggests that authenticity can be understood as relating not only to the language selected to be taught but the task on which the learner is engaged and the social setting which is created in the classroom. He expresses these distinctions as four types of authenticity:

1   Authenticity of the texts which we may use as input data for our students.
2   Authenticity of the learners' own interpretations of such texts.
3   Authenticity of tasks conducive to language learning.
4   Authenticity of the actual social situation of the classroom language.   *(1985: 61)*

This distinction enables Breen to say that 'inauthentic language-*using* behaviour might be authentic language-*learning* behaviour'. The difficulty with such a conclusion is that one can claim authenticity for anything that goes on in the classroom, including mechanistic pattern practice and the recital of verb paradigms, on the grounds that it may be conducive to learning (type 3) and a feature of the conventional classroom situation (type 4). This bears some resemblance to the definition of communication referred to in Chapter 2 and seems to me to generalize the meaning of the term authenticity to the point where it ceases to have much significance. I would prefer to retain the term to refer to the normal language behaviour of the user in pursuit of a communicative outcome rather than the language-like behaviour of the learner. Thus inauthentic language-using behaviour might well be *effective* language-learning behaviour, but to call the latter 'authentic' seems to me to confuse the issue.

However, the kind of enquiry which Breen conducts here, the interpretation and evaluation of ideas in reference to pedagogic issues, is a very good example of the process of appraisal that I am proposing. Its value lies in the way it opens up the issue for reasoned discussion.

The efficiency of natural learning. Whereas the means/end assumption leads to the promotion of authentic, natural communicative activity based on a belief in the determining effect of eventual purpose, the assumption of the efficiency of natural learning invokes the naturalness criterion in reference to the learning process itself. The former assumption says that language behaviour in the classroom has to be natural so as to conform to the naturalness of language use: the latter assumption says that classroom behaviour has to be natural in conformity with natural processes of language learning. Whereas the first assumption derives from ideas arising from descriptions of language use, the second derives from ideas emerging from second language acquisition (SLA) research.

Such research is concerned with the identification and explanation of developmental stages in the language acquisition process, with the determinants of natural learning. The assumption is that if such research is successful, then pedagogy is a matter of conforming to the revealed sequence of natural acquisition and of setting up conditions in the classroom which replicate those of its emergence. What this amounts to, in Corder's words, is 'the accommodation of the structure of our linguistic syllabuses and teaching materials to fit what is known of the sequence of progressive complication of the approximative systems of the free learner.' (1981: 77)

Note the term 'accommodation'. Note, too, that such an idea runs counter to the suggestion that syllabuses should be designed along notional/functional lines. The implications for pedagogy of SLA research on the one hand, and studies of communication on the other, come into conflict and so stand in particular need of conceptual evaluation. Corder's proposal also makes the equation between description and prescription which I questioned earlier. Descriptions of 'free' learning sequences cannot automatically determine the structure of contrived instruction any more than can descriptions of attested language use. I shall take this point up again in Chapters 9 and 10.

At all events SLA research, though of considerable theoretical and descriptive interest, has yielded as yet nothing definitive upon which one might confidently model an approach to formal teaching which replicates the process of natural learning (see Chapter 2). What we have are, in the words of T.S. Eliot, 'only hints and guesses / Hints followed by guesses'. These suggest the importance of giving primacy to communicative fluency rather than to formal accuracy (see Brumfit 1984a).

But even if definitive results were forthcoming, why should it be assumed as self-evident that natural learning is necessarily the most effective? Most of human progress seems to have come about by making the contrary assumption that nature can be improved upon by artifice of one kind or another. Social institutions, including that of education, are set up to counteract the shortcomings of nature, to control and exploit it and turn it to human advantage. The very concept of pedagogy (whether defined as art or science) presupposes invention and intervention which will direct learners in ways they would not, left to their own devices, have the opportunity or inclination to pursue. Now clearly a teaching approach which goes against the grain of natural disposition will create needless difficulties for the learner, as I pointed out earlier in reference to translation and the focusing on form, but it does not follow that pedagogy must therefore simply accommodate that disposition.

3   Operation

Operation is that part of the mediation process which is most readily recognized by teachers as their business. It is here that techniques of various kinds are put into action to achieve practical learning outcomes.

These techniques may be the conscious application of ideas which have been subjected to previous appraisal and are therefore the realization of principles, or they may simply be a set of more or less formulaic activities sanctioned not by appraisal but by the approval of authority. In the latter case, operation may simply be a matter of conforming to standard practices established by collective experience over time. Teacher preparation would then be mainly an initiation, learning the tricks of the trade from the old campaigners. Or perhaps authority may come from some prestigious source external to the domain of the practitioner, as when techniques are recommended on the grounds that they have the warrant of proven theory. On the one hand we have an internal authority which directs techniques to the maintenance of traditional practices, and on the other we have an external authority which directs techniques to the implementation of change. It is not surprising that they come into conflict, with one side feeling threatened by innovative theory and the other feeling frustrated by established practice.

From the point of view of teacher activity as pragmatic mediation, operational techniques are the enactment of ideas previously subjected to appraisal which provides them with a rationale. It may well be that there are good reasons for following customary practices or for rejecting them in favour of new ones, but teachers ought to know what these reasons are, for it is this knowledge which provides for adaptability, the alternative realization of principles through techniques appropriate to different instructional settings. Particular activities in the form of classroom tasks may appear to be very different and to represent quite distinct views of pedagogy but on closer consideration to be consistent with the same underlying principle of approach. Conversely, activities which seem on the surface to be the same may turn out to realize different underlying assumptions. A parallel might be drawn here with the process of translation. The ability to recast an expression from one language into the form of another depends on reference to some underlying construct of meaning which may establish a resemblance between expressions which appear very different and a distinction between expressions which appear to resemble each other. So it is with principles identified by evaluation and the techniques which put them into operation. In both translation and pedagogy, I suggest, effective mediation depends on the recognition of the relationship between underlying ideas and the surface forms which give them expression.

The conflicts that I referred to earlier commonly occur at the level of technique when operation is implemented in dissociation from appraisal, in the form, for example, of prescribed teaching materials which have the appearance of novelty. This has the effect of creating an opposition between established custom within which teachers feel secure and new ways which they are under pressure to adopt in the interests of progress. The result is a crisis of confidence, often resolved by teachers returning to the assurance of tradition which represents, after all, the more influential authority of the culture in which they have been nurtured.

But such conflicts can often be resolved and the oppositions reconciled, at least to some degree, at the level of principle. As I indicated earlier, the process of appraisal necessarily entails reference to established ideas and the balancing of the competing forces of assimilation and accommodation. It follows that any proposal for change would be referred to customary ways of thinking, and this provides for the possibility of operational techniques which realize new ideas being devised as an extension of existing practices. Thus the damaging divide between what is established and what is innovative is avoided, the present is seen to be an evolution from the past and not an abrupt and revolutionary change of paradigm which requires a radical shift in allegiance.

Notice that appraisal, stimulated by new ideas, does not necessarily undermine conventional assumptions and practices. It may indeed confirm them. But it will do so by making them explicit, so that in effect techniques become distinguishable from the principles which inform them. In this way, conventional practices are rationalized and so made more adaptable, as both Brumfit and Krashen point out.

It is quite common to hear teachers say that they do not subscribe to any particular approach or method in their teaching but are 'eclectic'. They thereby avoid commitment to any current fad that comes up on the whirligig of fashion. This might be regarded as prudent common sense. But if by eclecticism is meant the random and expedient use of whatever technique comes most readily to hand, then it has no merit whatever. It is indeed professionally irresponsible if it is claimed as a pedagogic principle. 'Haphazard' rather than 'eclectic' would be the more accurate term. If eclecticism is to be a matter of principle, it cannot apply independently at the level of operational technique: it must apply at the level of appraisal which techniques will make variably operational in the manner previously discussed. Eclectic techniques in this case will realize an underlying consistency. This does not mean that they must directly and uniquely derive from one particular model or method, excluding all others. This is where I consider Krashen, for example, is mistaken. He has harsh words to say about eclecticism. In so far as he means the random use of techniques removed from all contact with appraisal, then I think that he is right. But he appears to reject eclecticism as an evaluative principle as well and to argue that pedagogic practice must be the application of a single theory of language acquisition, namely his own. (See Chapter 2.) Indeed Krashen's work as a whole reveals very little in the way of appraisal as I have defined the concept: ideas are hurried through the processes of interpretation and evaluation and made operational as rapidly as possible. Thus eclecticism is avoided at the very stage in the process where it is most needed. The teacher is persuaded into conformity, submits to authority and is effectively discouraged from engaging in the process of pragmatic mediation which, I argue, defines the very profession of pedagogy.

4 Empirical evaluation

I use the term 'empirical evaluation' to mean formative evaluation in the sense of Scriven (1967). My own term is intended to reflect the research orientation of this activity. It is to be distinguished from summative evaluation, which I associate with assessment, a periodic measurement rather than a continuous monitoring of process. My view of the function of evaluation within the learning/teaching process is the same as that of Breen and Candlin, who comment:

> Evaluation within and of the curriculum can be a powerful and guiding force. Judgements are a crucial part of knowledge, learning and any educational process. By applying judgements to the curriculum itself, evaluation by the users of that curriculum can be brought into the classroom, evaluation can be made to serve as a basis for new directions in the process of teaching and learning . . . it can shape and guide learning and guide decisions within the curriculum process.
> *(1980: 105–6)*

Notice that both teacher *and* learner are seen as evaluators, a view I subscribe to (see also Alderson 1985).

Here we are concerned with how the effects of teaching techniques on learner behaviour are monitored and how the techniques are modified accordingly. Empirical evaluation differs from assessment, as the term is generally understood, in that it focuses not on the measurement of learner attainment as matched against norms or criteria of success but on the process of learning and the factors which appear to influence it. It is therefore a continuous enquiry into the relationship between teaching and learning as it is enacted in particular classroom contexts. As an integral part of the mediation model I have proposed, it can, of course, only be carried out by the individual teacher. This means that guidance for carrying out the task has to be provided in programmes of teacher preparation. Just what form such guidance might take is a question I shall return to in Chapter 4.

Notice that empirical evaluation has implications both for the operation and the conceptual evaluation phases of our scheme, as is indicated by the arrows in the diagram on page 32. When techniques are applied in the classroom and their effects are monitored, the question arises as to whether and to what extent these effects call for an adjustment of the techniques as realizations of a particular principle, or for a reappraisal of the principle itself. This (as I indicated earlier) is the pedagogic version of the researcher's dilemma in general: at what point does a researcher decide that the hypothesis is untenable in its present form and needs to be revised? The problem is one which cannot ultimately be resolved in pedagogy but it needs to be recognized, not in negative terms as a licence either for imposing fixed ideas or for random expediency, but as a positive incentive for continuing enquiry, which will be sensitive to the circumstances of different learning/teaching situations.

Evaluation looks at the relationship between teaching and learning: it therefore, logically enough, engages the participation of both teachers and learners. This, again, distinguishes evaluation from assessment. With assessment learners simply provide behavioural outputs: they are a source of data. They are not invited to enquire into the process of their learning or how this is affected by what teachers require them to do. With evaluation, as I conceive it here, they take on a more active monitoring role and, albeit under the ultimate direction of the teacher, become partners in the pedagogic enterprise. Their attitudes to teaching and their conceptions of the effects of classroom activities are taken into account. The teacher's evaluation of the effectiveness of a technique will depend in part on the way the learners evaluate its effects. It will not just be a matter of noting what linguistic behaviour it provokes.

Evaluation, then, is to be distinguished from the measurement of learner achievement. It is also to be distinguished from the measurement of method. By this I mean schemes that have been devised in the past to establish the efficacy of a particular approach to teaching. These necessarily seek to cancel out particularities in the interest of identifying a set of determining principles. The peculiarities of teachers and learners as interacting participants are eliminated as intervening variables, and the evaluation is done by avoiding the mediation process which I have been outlining. The evaluation I have in mind, as an intrinsic element in pragmatic pedagogy, is itself a function of teacher mediation and seeks to plot a course through the variables of particular classroom encounters. Its purpose is not to prove the efficacy of any particular method but to use a set of principles as bearings for the development of different techniques.

My purpose in this chapter has been to propose a model of language teaching and to show the interrelationship between its different elements. It is the activation of this interrelationship which defines teaching as a mediation process. But as I indicated in Chapter 1, and is apparent from subsequent discussion, such a definition represents teaching as essentially a research activity. We need now to consider the question of the nature of pedagogic research, how it differs from other kinds of research activity, and what implications arise from such considerations for the education of teachers. These matters are taken up in the next chapter.

4 Pedagogic research and teacher education

Researchers and teachers

Research is commonly taken to be the specialist and reserved occupation of theorists, an activity which is carried out in detachment from the immediacy of actual events and requiring knowledge and expertise of a kind which only academic intellectuals can legitimately claim to have. The activity yields findings which have the weight of authority and the stamp of truth. This view of research in respect of language teaching has, as I showed in Chapter 2, led to an unfortunate separation of roles which has proved damaging to the pedagogic cause: the researcher as the producer of truth on the one hand, and the language teacher as a consumer of it on the other. The paradoxical effect of this has been to put the researcher, including the one who claims to be working within applied linguistics, at a remove from the only contexts of application which can provide substantiating evidence for the relevance of the research. At the same time, the people who create these contexts, the teaching practitioners, are often made to feel that their own experience as pedagogic providers is not given sufficient recognition but is, on the contrary, misprized as lacking in rigour: wisdom which leads to understanding is overridden by knowledge which leads to explanation. The consequence of this division of roles is the kind of distrust and absence of fruitful collaboration which marks any lack of reciprocal relationship between cultures (of which more later). What is needed, then, is a concept of research and teaching which will bring them together into reciprocal dependence and so reconcile the requirements of relevance and rigour. The model of pragmatic mediation that I am proposing here is designed to meet that need.

The nature of research

To clarify how the model outlined in the previous chapter relates to, and draws upon, research as it is academically defined, it will be helpful to start by considering the nature of research in general terms. The range of activities carried out under its name is very diverse and different in kind, from armchair theorizing to the detailed accumulation and analysis of data, from metaphysical speculation to psychometric measurement. What they all have in common is that they are all attempts to go beyond appearances. They all seek, in their different ways, to discover abstract categories and connections underlying familiar phenomena. The basic motivation of all research is the conviction that things are not just as they appear to be, but are examples of covert categories and relations of one sort or another. What research does is to reformulate the familiar so that it assumes a new significance. Once such a formulation is proposed then it can of course be applied to other phenomena (other than those originally used) and these are explained as additional instances of the abstractions that have been established. Moreover, the specification of new categories and relations provides the means for manipulating phenomena by giving their underlying features a realization which is not currently attested. Thus discovery leads to invention. Research enables people to be aware of different ways of conceiving of the familiar world and, if they act on the new conception, to alter or extend their customary ideas and practices. In this way research can be seen as a continuing dialectical process: actuality is formulated as an abstraction which in turn leads to a reformulation of actuality.

An obvious question arises from this: how do we know whether the particular reformulations of a given piece of research are valid or not? After all, one might dream up all kinds of outlandish ideas, and make them look good by persuasive argument decked out in the trappings of authority and the careful selection of data. There are plenty of historical precedents for this, as I pointed out in Chapter 2. What they show is that no matter how objective or impartial enquiries may seek or claim to be they are always in some degree preconceived because they are preconditioned by cultural assumptions of one sort or another. The very conditions of systematic enquiry make this unavoidable. For such enquiry is based on idealization, the extraction of what is seen as essential from observable data, and idealization obviously cannot be free of ideological influence: it must be related to some pre-existing framework of belief. In other words, research is bounded by the same sort of conditions which bear on appraisal, as discussed above. Researchers enquire selectively into what they believe to be essential according to their conceptual bent, leaving the rest aside as incidental. Thus they are naturally predisposed to find what they are looking for. How, then, can validity be established?

Validity is a relative concept. Its relativity is a function of degrees of cultural affinity, the extent to which the informing disposition of the researcher is shared by others within the community to which he belongs. Although a researcher in a particular discipline, that is to say in a particular academic culture, will work within conventions of enquiry defined by that discipline, these will obviously in part be shared by other disciplines and in part shared also by the wider community within which the academic culture is located. The situation here is a familiar one in anthropology: the recognition of degrees of commonality of attitude and belief which provides for the variable definition of what constitutes cultural boundaries.

So it is that we can apply to research of different disciplinary provenance general criteria of appraisal approved by the wider culture of intellectual enquiry. There are two kinds of general criteria. One of these is conceptual and bears on the logical coherence of theory. The other is empirical and bears on the way the data of actuality are used to substantiate the theory. Thus in relation to conceptual criteria, research might be criticized on the grounds of inconsistency of reasoning or imprecision of terminology or general intellectual ineptitude, using the standards of argumentation approved by our culture (though not necessarily by others). The employment of these general conceptual criteria is central to the process of interpretation, as discussed in Chapter 3. As I indicated there, their employment is often prevented, however, by too ready an assimilation of ideas. If ideas sound good and meet the needs of a current state of affairs, they will tend to be accepted in some simple assimilable form without being subjected to scrutiny. With regard to empirical criteria, research can be criticized on the grounds of faulty methodology in the design of instruments for assembling data or in the means used for measuring them. Whereas conceptual criteria relate to how the abstraction has been formulated empirical criteria relate to how the abstraction is actualized in data.

These general criteria apply at the interpretation phase of the pragmatic process I am proposing here. But evaluation calls for more particular consideration and a closer look at the cultural differences between the domain of disciplines concerned with language and learning and the domain of the subject of language as it appears on the curriculum.

I have already discussed the more particular validation of ideas as they bear upon issues in language pedagogy in terms of the evaluation of principles in respect to transfer value. Conceptual criteria, then, as they are more specifically invoked to establish relevance across cultures or domains (from linguistics and other disciplines to language pedagogy), are used in the process of appraisal. The more particular examination of validity in respect of empirical criteria, however, has to do with the evaluation of techniques since it is these which refer abstractions back to actuality. Empirical criteria have to do with the process of application. But the pedagogic methodology of application is not the same kind of operation as the conventional research methodology of selective observation and controlled experiment.

The methodology of teaching and research

There are two ways in which a theoretical abstraction can be matched against the actuality which it claims to account for. One of them involves the observation of events as they actually occur, and the other involves experimentation which causes events to take place. Both operations are exercises in data control: the former by selection, the latter by manipulation. A good deal of observational research has been done on what goes on in classrooms, including language classrooms. Lessons have been analysed according to descriptive schemes of different sorts based on the abstraction of what the researchers have considered to be the most salient or significant features of classroom behaviour. In such classroom research, the teacher is part of the data to be observed. Work of a manipulative kind has also been done by using classes of learners as subject, but it is not the teacher, in her normal teaching role, who conducts the enquiry in these cases. If she is not data she is an intervening variable to be eliminated. Either way she is not in charge.

But in their professional role, teachers *are*, of course, in charge: they are not intervening variables but intervening agents.

Their business is to manipulate behaviour. Unlike the experimenter, however, they cannot, because of their prior responsibility to their pupils, simply eliminate or neutralize aspects of the learning milieu which are inconvenient for the conduct of experiment. Some of these aspects may well combine in complex and inexplicable ways in the learning process and clearly the teacher cannot take the chance of depriving learners of effective learning conditions on the grounds that they cannot be explained or controlled. The people in her charge are pupils and not experimental subjects. The teacher is accountable in a way that the experimenter is not: her purpose is to promote the understanding of her pupils and not, except incidentally, her own. Futhermore, as participants in the learning/teaching operation, pupils have a role in the evaluation process, as I pointed out earlier. They do not just generate data but enter into collaboration in the continuous monitoring of classroom activity and its effects.

There is, then, a difference between 'outsider' research (whether observational or manipulative) which is carried out by the external researcher with teachers as part of the data or the object of enquiry, and 'insider' research which is carried out by teachers themselves. We might refer to the former as 'classroom-oriented research' (see Seliger and Long 1983) and the latter as 'classroom-centred research' (see Allwright 1983). How far these two perspectives presuppose different procedures of enquiry is a matter of considerable current debate (see, for example, Mitchell 1985; van Lier 1988). One view is that insider research calls for the free-ranging exploration of what goes on in the classroom without the constraint of any preconceived theory. Such a view would, of course, be in conflict with the model I am proposing here, which involves the teacher in the experimental application of ideas.

But at the same time, the classroom cannot simply be an extension of the experimental domain. The empirical evaluation of teaching/learning activities does not aim at the exact specification of causes but at increased awareness of different factors which bear upon the learning process in particular classrooms. Certain generalities might well emerge, certain principles may be borne out, and these can form the basis for discussion with other teachers working in different circumstances, and the basis for variable realization as different techniques, as I indicated earlier. But classroom practice is not put at the service of the principles, designed to test them out; conversely, the principles serve classroom practices in that they provide a way in which they may be more clearly understood and more systematically carried out.

The point I am making is that pedagogic research calls for the independent appraisal of ideas as a precondition to their application. That application cannot simply model itself on the procedures of empirical research, however, since it has to operate within contexts which preclude it. This does not mean that these procedures cannot be adapted to classroom use. Indeed, it may be that the best approach to the design of guidelines for empirical evaluation is to begin with familiar and well-tried procedures for the elicitation and observation of data and see how far they can be adapted to serve a pedagogic purpose. A comparative study of research procedures and teaching techniques would be likely to provide a basis for evaluation which combines the qualities of research rigour and pedagogic relevance.

The value of using observational research procedures for the purpose of evaluation is indicated by Long in the following terms:

> It should be stressed that the aim in providing teachers with training in observational procedures is not to turn them into classroom researchers . . . Rather, the idea is to equip them to assess what they are doing when back in the field, and to monitor any innovations they make in their teaching. *(1983b: 288)*

Long gives a number of instances of such procedures. The interesting question, in the present context, is how far these can be co-ordinated with familiar pedagogic techniques, thereby bringing research within the compass of normal teaching; or, in more general terms, what implications does work on classroom observation have for developments in teacher education (see Allwright 1988).

One further observation might be made about pedagogic research. The idea that teachers should adopt a research perspective in their teaching has been current in educational thinking (in Britain at least) for a good number of years, associated in particular with the work of Stenhouse and Elliott (for example, Stenhouse 1975; Elliott 1981). The term 'action research' is used to refer to such research-oriented teaching. But this is sometimes taken to mean the formation of groups of teachers to generate their own ideas without reference to theory and research of a more rigorous and academic character. 'Be your own expert' is sometimes the cry and the do-it-yourself attitude extends to educational thinking. This, it seems to me, is symptomatic of a dangerous anti-intellectual trend in the profession. I have been arguing here for what might be termed appropriate research, analagous to the notion of appropriate technology. But this does not mean that it has to be uninformed and makeshift. The academic disciplines of linguistics, psychology, sociology, and education provide the essential bearings for the professional teacher both in the ideas they generate and in their processes of enquiry, and it is the task of applied linguistics (whose name belies its scope) to make the insights these disciplines offer accessible for appraisal and application. The kind of pragmatic approach to pedagogy that I have outlined here depends on the recognition of the importance of intellectual effort and puts theoretical rigour at the service of practical relevance.

It is perhaps worth saying again that this argument for a rational basis for pedagogy does not imply that everything about good teaching can be reduced to what is rational. There is no denial of the value of imagination and intuition, the instinctive feel for what is effective. As Brumfit observes, 'Being a good teacher is never exactly the same thing as understanding teaching; there are many things we can do well that we cannot fully understand.' (1987: 29) I would only add that the value of what we cannot understand is only recognized by reference to what we can. The principles of pedagogy have to do with the *craft* of teaching. They cannot account for the *artistry* of the individual practitioner. On the other hand, individual artistry is likely to be enhanced by an increased consciousness of craft.

The research-oriented approach to teaching that I have been proposing here obviously sets a high premium on teacher preparation, and that in turn raises the issues of the education and training of teachers.

The education and training of teachers

How can teachers be prepared to undertake the process of pragmatic mediation that I have been proposing in these chapters? The requirement for a research perspective which this necessarily entails, the relating of abstraction to actuality, the use of technique to realize principle, and indeed the whole process of self-monitoring, presupposes attitudes and abilities which call for the education and not just the training of teachers. Indeed, as I have already indicated, it seems to me that the very claim of pedagogy to professional status is based on the same supposition. What then does teacher education involve and how does it differ as a concept from teacher training?

In general terms, the distinction between education and training can be formulated in the following way. Training is a process of preparation towards the achievement of a range of outcomes which are specified in advance. This involves the acquisition of goal-oriented behaviour which is more or less formulaic in character and whose capacity for accommodation to novelty is, therefore, very limited. Training, in this view, is directed at providing solutions to a set of predictable problems and sets a premium on unreflecting expertise. It is dependent on the stability of existing states of affairs since it assumes that future situations will be predictable replicas of those in the past. Education on the other hand is not predicated on predictability in this way. It provides for situations which cannot be accommodated into preconceived patterns of response but which require a reformulation of ideas and the modification of established formulae. It focuses, therefore, not on the application of ready-made problem-solving techniques but on the critical appraisal of the relationship between problem and solution as a matter of continuing enquiry and of adaptable practice. For further discussion see Peters 1967, 1973; Widdowson 1983, and with particular reference to language teaching, Larsen-Freeman 1983.

It should be noted that this view of teacher education does not give warrant to abstract speculation for its own sake in dissociation from actuality. Rather it provides for the initiative of invention whereby actuality can be variously interpreted and changed. This does not mean that the educated teacher will continually be in quest of innovation and reject conventional practices out of hand. It means only that ideas both given and new will be subjected to scrutiny and not simply accepted on trust. The reason for the familiar bandwagon phenomenon is to be found in educational failure.

Teacher education, then, provides for the appraisal of ideas in order to make them more practically effective, because an understanding of abstract concepts and their relationships allows for adaptability in their realization. It follows that such an educational perspective on teacher preparation does not deny the importance of practical technique. On the contrary, it proclaims its crucial role as effecting a renewal of connection with the actuality of particular classrooms contexts. But techniques are not goals in themselves, as they are in a training perspective; they are the means for making ideas operational and subject to modification in the light of evaluation. They do not determine the activities of teaching and learning, but on the contrary are themselves required to conform to the changing perceptions and experiences of the teacher and learner.

The way techniques are to be considered in teacher education, not as procedures to conform to but to exploit, bears on the question of the use of existing teaching materials in the preparation of teachers. These teaching materials are techniques made manifest by the specific choice of language, designed and arranged as a series of tasks or exercises for immediate implementation. To the extent that such materials are realizations of principles, instances of what exercises informed by certain ideas might look like, then they are illustrations. They can be assessed by reference to abstractions. To the extent that such materials are designed for direct implementation with the implicit claim for general pedagogic effectiveness, then they are prescriptions. They presuppose that the particularities of different classrooms are not determinants of teaching and learning but are incidental. In this case, they can only be assessed by reference to actuality.

As illustrations, therefore, teaching materials can be seen as stimulants of enquiry calling for appraisal as a prerequisite for application; as prescriptions, they call for application without the requirement of appraisal, and so constrain the users into conformity. A training perspective would obviously tend towards the prescription view of teaching materials, an educational perspective would require the treatment of such materials as illustrations.

This distinction between the illustrative and prescriptive character of teaching materials, though obvious enough, does not always seem to be recognized. The materials which I designed myself as illustrative of a particular approach to teaching (for example, Widdowson 1978; Allen and Widdowson 1973), have been criticized on the grounds that they have not been subjected to evaluation and thereby given the seal of practical effectiveness (Murphy 1985). But the point about the evaluation of materials is that it cannot be carried out in dissociation from the contexts of particular classrooms: it must be part of the process of self-monitoring mediation that I am advocating here. In this view there can be no possibility of any global approval or rejection. It is interesting to note that Murphy's concept of evaluation in this respect is at variance with that of Breen and Candlin which I referred to earlier.

I have talked so far about teacher training and education without distinguishing between pre-service and in-service programmes. It seems reasonable to suppose that there will be differences in the kind of provision that needs to be made by each of these stages of teacher formation. These differences are, I believe, closely related to the training and education perspectives outlined above.

Pre-service preparation initiates the prospective teacher into the basics of professional activity. These are, in general, of two kinds. There are those which relate to the craft of classroom management and the use of routine procedures for organizing class activity, the tricks of the pedagogic trade. Here what is important for novices is the development of confidence when confronted with a new and demanding, indeed threatening, social situation, and for this they need to draw upon a set of established and reliable techniques and learn to feel secure in the straightforward business of actually putting them into practice, whatever their validity in terms of learning effect might be. Novice teachers clearly have to feel secure in their own role, and establish their own identity, before indulging in experimentation which could undermine their authority before they have actually acquired it.

The second basic element of initiation is that which relates newcomers to their fellow teachers, a process of acculturation whereby they become members of the group. This too inclines them to accept a set of conventional attitudes and practices. To adopt too critical or enquiring a position at this stage would be to run the risk of alienation. In their initiation into both the craft and culture of pedagogy, it is in the interests of novice teachers to conform in order to place their relations with pupils and fellow teachers on a secure base and so to get established in their role. In view of this, it seems clear that pre-service or initial preparation needs to pay particular attention to training. This is not to say that such courses would not also encourage an awareness of wider theoretical implications or the kind of appraisal I have associated with education, but this would be more in the manner of a long-term investment rather than something expected to yield immediate returns, something which might influence attitude rather than instigate action.

The instigation of action, indeed of action research, is a matter which must mainly be taken up by in-service provision. And it is here, of course, that an educational orientation is required in order that teachers might enact the role of mediator along the lines I have been proposing. There is, of course, very extensive provision already made in the field of in-service education for language teachers, ranging from award-bearing year-long courses in universities to the relatively informal meetings of teacher groups on a self-help basis. With such programmes there is, however, a persistent problem of renewal of connection with the classroom. This is perhaps more evident in the case of longer courses where teachers are displaced from their pedagogic habitat for considerable periods of time, but it exists also in shorter courses. What happens very often here is that participants are inspired by the social and professional intensity of the event but find that they have little to carry home with them except a heady sense of general enlightenment which is often quickly dispersed on its contact with reality. This is not to deny the value of such courses: they provide, at the very least, a sense of professional community and there is no doubt that some of the inspiration they generate carries over into practice. But for many participants what is needed is something more definite in the way of a scheme of work of some kind which will direct and maintain the momentum of the course into a continuing programme of monitored activities in the classroom. It seems to me that it should be the purpose of all in-service courses to develop such schemes through the joint enterprise of the participants. In this way, these courses prepare teachers for the responsibility of their own continuing professional education. They are provided with guidance which enables them to take the initiative.

I would now like to make specific proposals as to how the model of pragmatic mediation that I have proposed in these chapters might be made operational within a programme of in-service education for language teachers.

Model to module

I have presented the rationale for a pragmatic approach to language pedagogy which casts the teacher in the role of mediator between theory and practice. I have tried to show how such an approach is necessary if language teaching is to draw maximal benefits from developments in the informing disciplines while retaining its own identity as a domain of enquiry which has to meet its own conditions of relevance and accountability. And I have indicated some of the negative consequences of pragmatic failure.

The adoption of this model of pedagogy means that the teacher is necessarily engaged in research as an aspect of teaching and this research too has its own character and its own criteria of relevance and success. It carries with it, too, implications for teacher preparation. The conduct of pedagogic research as I have defined it here presupposes attitudes and approaches to techniques of teaching which are developed only through an educational perspective and this in turn calls for a continuous programme of in-service support. Such continuity can only be assured by the design of schemes of work which constitute guidelines for classroom action.

What I have in mind are portfolios or fascicules of data and tasks representing modules of enquiry which deal with issues of current pedagogic concern in a format which, being based on the pragmatic model that I have proposed, draws the teacher into the appraisal and application of ideas. The starting-point is not a theoretical insight or a research finding or a recommended line of approach but what the teacher finds problematic, what issues are from her point of view in need of clarification and resolution. Generally speaking, we know all too little about the teacher's perspective on pedagogy; we make generalizations which are not based on anything in the way of reliable information. We are very prone to pontificate about what teachers *should* think about but we do not really know what they *do* think about: we formulate issues on their behalf. What is needed is an investigation into what language teachers in different classrooms in different countries find problematic about conventional practice or about proposals for innovation that have been put forward. Modules could then be directed at issues which teachers themselves see as of central concern.

In the current absence of information about problematic

matters from the teachers' point of view, one can only make assumptions based on impressions about the kind of issue that is uppermost in their minds. The following might be suggested as possibilities for the purpose of illustration.

Structure practice

Conventional wisdom supports the use of drills, substitution tables, and other devices for pattern practice on the grounds that they make a knowledge of language forms habitual. Recent ideas about language use and learning insist on the primacy of communicative activities in the classroom. Does this mean that conventional ways are mistaken and should be abandoned? Is there any place for practice exercises in a communicative approach to language teaching?

Learner error

It has been suggested that learner errors can be seen as evidence of learner achievement. Does this mean that they should not be corrected under any circumstances? If there *are* circumstances where error correction is legitimate, what are they, and how does the teacher set about it without inhibiting learner development?

Authentic materials

It has been traditionally supposed that the language presented to learners should be simplified in some way for easy access and acquisition. Nowadays there are recommendations that the language presented should be authentic. How is it to be graded so that it can be made accessible? Is simplification as a pedagogic strategy inconsistent with the principles of a communicative approach to language teaching?

The first stage in module design, then, is the identification of problems from the teacher's point of view. These may be formulated in more or less specific terms and the rather general issues that I have already outlined may be broken down into more narrowly focused questions and be dealt with in more than one module with provision made for explicit cross-reference. In the case of *structure practice*, for example, more specific issues might be:

Are meaningful drills possible?
What is the function of substitution tables?

How do language exercises differ from communicative tasks?

Modules might then be designed which deal separately with each question but which have elements in common in respect to underlying aspects of appraisal. In this way, the more specific question would be related to a more comprehensive framework of conceptual evaluation, and particular techniques seen to be realizations of more general principles of teaching. The relative narrowness of focus of particular modules, and the way this corresponds with the need for cross-reference to make explicit the common denominator of principle, are matters which cannot be determined in advance but depend on what teachers conceive their problems to be and on the actual experience of designing and using such modules.

After identification of the problem to be addressed, the next stage is to draw attention to ideas which bear upon it for interpretation and conceptual evaluation. This might best be done by a judicious selection of quotations which teachers would be guided to study in detail. The original problem could then be reconsidered in the light of this appraisal and the next stage would be to move into application, making the ideas operational by the teacher's devising activities in reference to given examples drawn from existing teaching materials. These would subsequently be tried out and evaluated in the classroom, the teacher having been given a set of possible procedures for doing this. The following schematic sketch will give some indication of what modules designed along these lines might look like.

Outline module: drills and meaning

Problem:	To know whether the use of drills is consistent with the teaching of meaning. Are meaningful drills a contradiction in terms?
Appraisal:	Appropriate quotations from (for example):

Richards *et al.* 1984	for definition of terms
Rivers 1964	
Dakin 1973	on the nature and use of drills in language teaching
Palmer 1981	on the nature of meaning
Yule 1985	

By consideration of points raised in the module, and matters arising from them, teachers are made aware of the distinction between drills promoting mechanistic performance and drills promoting the unconscious internalization of mentalistic competence structures, and of the distinction between meaning as semantic signification and meaning as pragmatic value in context.

Conclusions emerging from conceptual evaluation: types of drill can in principle be associated with types of meaning. They can be used with a problem-solving element to develop a knowledge of semantic meaning as signalled by lexis and syntax within sentences and can be used in support of tasks which focus on pragmatic meaning by providing a consciousness-raising extension to communication-oriented activities.

Application: Sample drills provided, selected from existing materials with reference to procedural guidance. Versions of these to be used in class. Feedback in respect of learner attitude and achievement to be recorded. Exercises adjusted accordingly.

I have given only a very rough and general indication of how the model of teacher mediation I have presented and argued for in this chapter might itself be made operational. The detailed design of individual modules will need careful thought and will need to respond to the problems which teachers themselves recognize as important. Furthermore, since they are not directives but guidelines they must be flexible enough to allow for teacher participation and the exercise of initiative so that teachers can follow their course in reference to the bearings provided. These modules are like the data and suggestions provided for project work and are therefore incomplete. In using them in classrooms and in discussing them with colleagues, teachers will change them, replace them, and develop their own, more immediate to their own teaching circumstances. They have, in this sense, an essentially catalytic character.[1] Their

---

[1] These modules, not surprisingly, bear a resemblance to the elements of the INSET scheme designed by C.N. Candlin and myself (see Anderson and Lynch 1988, Bygate 1987, Cook 1989, Malamah-Thomas 1987, Nunan 1988, Wright 1987:—all titles in *Language Teaching: A Scheme for Teacher Education.*) Although they are informed by the same rationale, these modules differ in that they are intended as kits or worksheets for separate mini-projects, are more specifically focused on particular topics and derive more directly from the perceptions of teachers. They are more individualized and local, more subject to modification in use.

function is to stimulate a pragmatic approach to teaching and teacher education.

In the chapters of this part of the book I have sought to provide a rationale for such an approach. If appraisal now reveals that it has some validity in principle, the next stage is application. And that is, of course, beyond the scope of this discussion.

PART TWO

Aspects of language

5 Preliminaries: approaches to description

The definition of teaching as a pragmatic process of continuous evaluation, as proposed in the previous chapter, does not, of course, apply only to the teaching of languages but is in principle applicable to the teaching of all subjects on the curriculum. We move on now to aspects of teaching of more particular concern to the language teacher, but as we do so we should not lose sight of the more general educational context. As will become apparent in subsequent chapters, many ideas relating to the teaching of languages have a more common currency across the curriculum—ideas like the creative classroom and task-based learning, for example, and the need to resolve the competing claims of teacher authority and learner autonomy. One might say, indeed, that recent developments in communicative language teaching have brought language teachers into closer alignment with their colleagues. But in this part of the book my purpose is more specifically to consider aspects of language and the extent to which they indicate how we are to define our particular subject.

Language and linguistics: subject and discipline

It seems reasonable to suppose that the definition of a language as a subject for learning should in some way be informed by theories about the nature of language in general on the one hand and by descriptions of languages in particular on the other. After all, we would be surprised if the subjects of physics or history were defined in disregard of theoretical ideas and descriptive facts coming from the scholarly disciplines which bear the same name. And so it seems self-evident that the subject of language should also draw on a cognate disciplinary source even though it happens in this case to have the different name of linguistics.

As I have already indicated, there are broadly speaking two

kinds of insight of potential relevance to language teaching which we might expect linguistics to provide. One comes from theory, and has to do with ideas about the nature of language in general as a psychological and social phenomenon, internalized in the mind, externalized in social life. The other comes from description, and provides information about the properties of particular languages as formal abstractions and as actualized in use.

It seems to be commonly supposed that it is description rather than theory as such which makes the most direct contribution to language teaching. For example:

> He [the language teacher] is not teaching linguistics. But he is teaching something which is the object of study of linguistics, and is described by linguistic methods. It is obviously desirable that the underlying description should be as good as possible, and this means that it should be based on sound linguistic principles.
>
> This is the main contribution that the linguistic sciences can make to the teaching of languages: to provide good descriptions . . . There is no conflict between application and theory; the methods most useful in application are to be found among those that are most valid and powerful in theory.
> *(Halliday et al. 1964: 166–67)*

Similarly, Corder, though sounding a note of caution about adopting too restrictive a model of description, expresses the view that pedagogy draws selectively from descriptions of language provided by linguistics. The difference is not qualitative but quantitative, a matter of selection only:

> Thus the descriptions of a language which are the output of a first-order application of linguistic theory represent only an inventory from which a *selection* must be made in order to draw up the syllabus for any particular teaching operation.
> *(1973: 143)*

Both of these views hold that the influence of linguistics on language teaching should be mediated through descriptions which are informed by theory. These descriptions—the first-order applications of theory, as Corder calls them—then serve as a source of information, an inventory of items, from which the language to be taught can be directly derived. In this view, teachers have no direct contact with theory, though it may be dimly discerned through the description.

Type and token descriptions of language

We should note that the description of a language in the terms of categories which theory provides may account either for *types* of linguistic element in the abstract, or for *tokens* of linguistic element as they actually occur in contexts of use. A description which deals with abstract types will present linguistic forms and their meanings as constituents of the conventional code. Where these forms are syntactic combinations of words, the result is a descriptive grammar like that of Quirk *et al.* (1972, 1985). With such descriptions, actually occurring linguistic data, where they are adduced at all, serve to exemplify category types. A description which deals with actual tokens of language use reveals the relative frequency of forms and their habitual co-occurrence in different contexts.

Thus a type description might present a comprehensive array of structures and give each of them equal descriptive weight, but a token description might well reveal that some of these were of rare occurrence, or restricted to a realization through a limited range of lexical items, almost exclusively confined to certain contexts, or associated with certain meanings.

Token descriptions on a massive scale are now possible with the development of the computer. The evidence they yield does not just quantify the token occurrence of existing category types, for the most part derived from intuition, but also suggests that the types themselves stand in need of revision so that the language as abstractly conceived by the linguist is brought into closer correspondence with the language as actually realized by the user.

The two kinds of description, then, take very different perspectives on language. The type description considers language as abstract knowledge, the token description as actual behaviour. The extent to which these approaches are complementary has to do with the relationship between competence and performance and is a matter of current debate. Sinclair, for example, is in no doubt that recent developments in what I have called token description require a radical revision of principles of descriptive procedure in general, and have profound implications for language pedagogy in particular:

> For some years I tended to assume that the computers would merely give us a better documented description of the language, but I do not think that that position remains tenable. Now that we have the means to observe samples of

language which must be fairly close to representative samples, the clear messages are:

a) We are teaching English in ignorance of a vast amount of basic fact. This is not our fault, but it should not inhibit the absorption of the new material.

b) The categories and methods we use to describe English are not appropriate to the new material. We shall need to overhaul our descriptive systems.

c) Since our view of the language will change profoundly, we must expect substantial influence on the specification of syllabuses, design of materials and choice of method.
   (1985: 252)

What Sinclair is saying is that type descriptions of language knowledge based on intuitive impression and not grounded in actually attested data do not provide an adequate source of reference for language teaching. What is required is that the language which is pedagogically presented should be a projection of that which actually occurs as recorded by the computer analysis of text.

I made the point earlier that descriptive facts about actual usage do not necessarily determine what is to be included in a language course. The abstractions of a type description may be preferred on occasions in that they activate more effectively the process of learning. Consider, for example, that type of syntactic structure which Chomsky refers to as the kernel sentence, of which the following are examples:

The birds are singing.
The farmer killed the duckling.

The likelihood is that such spare syntactic structures appear very infrequently as independent forms in actual use. But as Chomsky himself remarked when he abandoned them with some reluctance as theoretical constructs, these kernel sentences actually have considerable intuitive appeal. They seem to have a certain psychological reality for native speakers as units of knowledge in spite of their abnormality as units of behaviour. One might surmise that this is because they represent elemental features from which all other structures are compounded and so constitute basic units of mental processing from which all learning proceeds. Be that as it may, the intuitive reality of such structures is borne out also by the fact that generations of language teachers have recognized that they have a leading role to play in the initial stages of learning, because of what I have called their valency or combining power. Now generations of teachers may of course be wrong. But it will not do just to dismiss the evidence of their experience out of hand.

The relevance of linguistic theory

The point is that whether descriptions are knowledge or behaviour oriented, type or token, they cannot determine what the teacher does. They have always to be referred to pedagogic decision. But this decision will need to be informed by an understanding of what theoretical assumptions underlie the different descriptions. As we have seen, the usual belief is that what teachers need is descriptions, with the implication that they need not be bothered with the theoretical ideas upon which they are based. I should like to put the contrary view that an understanding of theory is of primary importance because this provides a general perspective on the nature of language which influences pedagogic principles and indicates how different descriptions might be adapted for classroom use. In other words, to refer back to the discussion in the previous section, an understanding of theory is needed for evaluation.

Theories about language, its development as a mental construct, and its operation in social life, have had an enormous influence on how teachers of second languages have conceived of their subject. The basic principles which have been adopted in these aspects of teaching which Sinclair mentions—'specification of syllabuses, design of materials and choice of method'—have been drawn not from particular descriptions of the language but from ideas, assumptions, and beliefs about language in general. It seems to me to be entirely right that this should be so. For although teachers will find descriptions in dictionaries and grammars of immense value as sources of reference, ultimately it will be up to them to decide on how theoretical ideas are to be applied and evaluated in the pedagogic treatment of language.

But if teachers are to take such decisions they need to have access to these ideas. This is in part what I hope to provide here in respect of certain current theoretical perspectives and pedagogic approaches. The two following chapters explore an issue which has been prominent in the debate on language teaching in recent years (and which is related to the distinction between type and token descriptions which I discussed above), namely the relationship between meaning as formally encoded in a language, its grammar and lexis, and meaning which is achieved in context by the exploitation of these formal properties.

It often seems to be supposed that a concern for grammar is inconsistent with the principles of communicative language teaching. This supposition is, I believe, based on an impoverished concept of the nature of grammar, one which does not account for the complementary functioning of lexis and syntax as an essential resource for the negotiation of meaning in context. In chapters 6 and 7 I would like to propose a characterization of grammar and language use which shows their interdependence.

6 Grammar, and nonsense, and learning

Nonsensical sentences

The title of this chapter comes from a song in Oliver Goldsmith's play *She Stoops to Conquer*, sung by Tony Lumpkin, a character who misspends much of his time in a tavern called 'The Three Pigeons':

> Let schoolmasters puzzle their brain
> With grammar, and nonsense, and learning . . .

In Tony Lumpkin's judgement, good liquor is much to be preferred to all this. But we cannot afford to be so self-indulgent and dismissive. Over recent years schoolteachers and others concerned with the teaching of languages have 'puzzled their brains' about the role of grammar in language learning, and some maintain that students can manage without it. Others have persisted in a more traditional view that language learning is essentially the same as the learning of grammar. So what is the relationship between the two?

Tony Lumpkin associates grammar with nonsense. He is not alone. No less a person than Firth, not someone, one supposes, who would have rejected all learning in favour of the bottle, observes that grammarians 'make regular use of nonsense'. He gives the example:

> I have not seen your father's pen, but I have read the book of your uncle's gardener. *(1957: 24)*

This, though exemplifying the syntax of English, is in Firth's view nonsensical as an expression of meaning. So, he asserts, are other rather less extreme examples, including the following, all of which appear as instances of English in books by reputable grammarians:

> The farmer killed the duckling.
> Pussy is beautiful.
> The lion roars.

Firth's strictures would, of course, apply equally to a very large number of sentences appearing in language teaching textbooks and practised by pupils. In this case, nonsense is not only associated with grammar but learning as well.

What Firth is pointing out is that sentences as artificial constructs for exemplifying linguistic forms do not meet the same conditions of making sense as do expressions naturally used in the service of communication in context. They have no 'implication of utterance': whatever meaning *potential* they might have is remote from any realization, since the contexts which would provide the occasion for their use are of unlikely occurrence. Of course, many people concerned with language teaching have come to a similar conclusion. In consequence, there has arisen a deep distrust of sentences and, by association, of the grammar they exemplify. But grammar cannot be equated with the devices used to exemplify its formal properties. There is more to it than that.

Let us begin by considering Firth's point more closely. It can be related to Sinclair's observation that examples of English are sometimes given which the analysis of actual data reveals do not in fact occur (see page 76). In both cases the objection is to the presentation of expressions *in* English as if they were normal uses *of* English. What is not clear, however, is the nature of the abnormality which is being objected to. Is it to do with the syntactic structure or to the way in which this structure is lexically manifested? One may agree that the expression which Firth dismisses as nonsense has a curious ring to it but this seems to be due to the choice of lexis which results in a particularly inconsequential proposition which it is hard to imagine ever figuring in actual use. If we alter the lexis, we can arrive at what would seem to be an entirely normal expression:

> I have not seen your father's pen, but I have read the book of your uncle's gardener.
> I have not seen your client's proposals, but I have read the report of your company's accountant.

It may be that this relexicalized version has not been actually attested and may never occur in the future but it acquires normality because it is relatively easy to conceive of a context for it. In this respect, the basic criterion for normality is not actual occurrence but contextual plausibility. And this is something which computer analysis of a corpus cannot of course determine.

Notice that the principle of contextual plausibility allows legitimacy to expressions which arise in the contrived contexts of the classroom. If it is allowed that such contrivance is pedagogically desirable as activating the process of learning, then it sets its own conditions for normality. The crucial point is that such expressions should be warranted by conceptual and communicative purposes recognized as having point in classroom activity. These purposes do not, however, have to correspond with those which are current or 'authentic' uses of language in the world at large. This matter will be taken up again in Section 3 of this book.

For the moment we need to notice that if normality is to be defined not in terms of contextual plausibility but in terms of frequency of attested occurrence, then in principle the teacher, selecting language by this criterion, would be confined to a presentation of expressions which realized a particular combination of syntactic elements with particular lexical items. Such combinations constitute formulaic patterns which are indeed of very frequent occurrence in language use and need to be accounted for (as I mentioned in Chapter 3) but they can hardly be said to represent the total language to be taught.

Grammar is clearly central to the working of language. But it is equally clear that its nature cannot be accounted for by demonstrating its rules by a random use of any lexical items that come to mind. I have suggested that it enters into some kind of relationship with words and contexts. Grammar is not just a collection of sentence patterns signifying nonsense, something for the learner's brain to puzzle over.

What is it then? And what is the nature of this relationship between words and contexts I have referred to? It is obviously important that we should have some clear idea about the nature of the phenomenon as an aspect of language not just as a preliminary but as a prerequisite for determining how it should figure in pedagogy.

One obvious way of finding out what grammar is is to look up the term in a dictionary. David Crystal has produced a work which ought to be particularly well suited to our purpose. It is called *A First Dictionary of Linguistics and Phonetics* (1980). Two pages are devoted to the entry *grammar*. Unfortunately they leave us little the wiser about its essential nature. It is, we are told (among other things) 'a systematic description of a language', 'the way words, and their component parts, combine to form sentences', 'a device for generating a finite specification of the sentences of a language'. So grammar is the name we give to the knowledge of how words are adapted and arranged to form sentences. And its operation can be exemplified by the kind of nonsensical expressions that Firth complains about. But what are sentences? One might demonstrate their formal properties but what are they actually *used* for? Why do words have to be subjected to adaptation and arrangement in this way?

Grammar, words, and context

There are after all occasions when words do very well on their own. Consider the classic case of the surgeon performing an operation and the utterances he addresses to his assistants: 'Scalpel!' 'Swab!' 'Clamp!' etc. No sign of grammar here: no interrogative forms, modal verbs, question tags; no sentence at all. Just words. The reason why communication is achieved here by lexical means only is of course because the context of shared knowledge makes it possible to use minimal cues. The conceptual or lexical meaning is sufficient for its indexical purpose on this occasion.

The notion of indexical meaning (which I have expounded in detail in Widdowson 1983, 1984a, and which I shall discuss again in Chapter 7) is crucial here. By 'indexical' I mean the function which is attributed to the linguistic sign by the language user when it occurs in context. It is used as an indicator or pointer to those features of the situation or existing knowledge that need to be engaged to realize meaning. Indexical meaning, achievable only pragmatically in reference to context, is contrasted with symbolic meaning which inheres in the linguistic sign as a stable semantic property. Thus the word *scalpel* has an established signification as a linguistic symbol recorded in the dictionary ('a small, thin, very sharp knife used for surgical dissection'). In the context of the operating theatre, the indexical use of the sign allows for the identification of a particular scalpel, and for the recognition that the surgeon is giving an order. 'Scalpel!', then, takes on the indexical value in this context of 'Pass me that particular scalpel'.

In this surgical context, the words are themselves sufficient as pointers to required meaning. Grammatical elaboration would be redundant. Indeed it would be dangerous: it would make communication less effective, the operation less efficient, and put the patient in peril. By the time the surgeon had produced his complete sentence, the patient might well have bled to death: a victim of syntax.

In this case words alone are enough to indicate meaning because of the high degree of contextual determinacy. On other occasions, indeed on most occasions, we cannot count on the context complementing words so closely, occasions when more precision is needed to identify the *contextual* features which are to be related to the *conceptual* meaning of the words to achieve indexical meaning. And this is where grammar comes in. Let us look again at the sentence that was cited earlier:

The farmer killed the duckling.

Stripped of its grammatical appendages and reduced to lexical essentials this appears as three words:

farmer kill duckling

The very conceptual meaning of these three lexical items in association allows us to infer a sort of unfocused proposition: a process *kill*, two participants in the process, one an agent, *farmer*, and the other a patient, *duckling*. Even if we were to change the linear arrangement, the three words presented in association would serve to indicate the same process and the same roles of the participants:

farmer duckling kill
duckling farmer kill
kill duckling farmer

In all these cases, our knowledge of what these words mean in English, and the very general context of our world knowledge would lead us to suppose that in all cases the farmer is the agent and the duckling at the receiving end of the action: the farmer does the killing and the duckling gets killed.

But let us now alter the lexis somewhat and consider the following three words in association:

hunter kill lion

We have the same process here, but now we cannot distinguish between the participant roles of *hunter* and *lion*. In the familiar world in which we live, ducklings are not known for their propensity for attacking farmers; they are classed among the victims of the killing process. But lions are a different matter.

Hunters might seek to kill them, but they are quite capable of turning the tables and acting out the agent role. There is nothing outlandish in the idea of lions killing hunters. So here the relationship between the lexical concepts has to be marked in some way to make up for the inadequacy of the words to indicate what part of the general context of knowledge is to be engaged. There are two possible states of affairs here, not just one. A common marking device used in English for such cases is word order. Since the mere association of words will not unambiguously point to meaning, the words need to be set down in a particular arrangement. Thus the sequence *hunter kill lion* signifies one thing, *hunter* agent, *lion* patient; *lion kill hunter* signifies the opposite, the *lion* as agent (the killer), the *hunter* as patient (the victim).

Word order is not the only conceivable grammatical device for enhancing the indexical precision of lexical items. One might use morphological rather than syntactic means. Many languages do. We might propose, for example, that the participant roles in our case might be marked by different suffixes: let us say *o* for the agent role, *om* for the patient. Word order would then not be needed for this particular purpose of role assignment. There would be *equivalence* of meaning with *different* word orders, as in:

huntero kill lionom
lionom kill huntero

And conversely, of course, *contrast* of meaning with the *same* word order:

huntero kill lionom
hunterom kill liono

Since word order is not now needed for signalling an increased specificity of conceptual meaning it can be put to other purposes, as we shall see presently.

But let us for the moment look at the word that signifies the process or action itself: the word *kill*. Again although there will be occasions when the bare lexical item will suffice to indicate meaning, when the context or the convergence of knowledge of those concerned will provide the specificity required, it will generally need to be supplemented by the addition of elements which give the word a more precise conceptual focus. We need devices for locating the process in time and for indicating its own temporal character. In other words, we need some way of marking tense and aspect. In English this is done by a combination of *addition* and *alteration*. The word is *altered* to signify present and past time:

> farmer kills duckling
> farmer killed duckling

And auxiliary verbs, themselves altered as necessary, are *added* to signify aspect:

> farmer is killing duckling
> farmer was killing duckling
> farmer has killed duckling
> farmer had killed duckling

In this way, the proposition is focused a little more clearly and its dependence on contextual support decreases accordingly. Again we should note that this increase in conceptual precision can be achieved, and is achieved in other languages, without recourse to grammatical devices of this kind. Lexical items might be used instead so that the focusing effect is brought about by extra words. We might propose something like the following for English: *then* and *now* for past and present; *be* and *have* for continuous and perfective:

> *then* farmer kill duckling = farmer kill*ed* duckling
> *now* farmer kill duckling = farmer kill*s* duckling
> *then* farmer *be* kill duckling = farmer *was* kill*ing* duckling
> *then* farmer *have* kill duckling = farmer *had* kill*ed* duckling
> *now* farmer *be* kill duckling = farmer *is* kill*ing* duckling
> *now* farmer *have* kill duckling = farmer *has* kill*ed* duckling

Marking for tense and aspect, then, are other communicative devices for getting features of context into focus, for providing a sharper definition of what words mean in relation to the external world. But we do not only report on events as they actually occur, we also make judgements about them, and we can call them into existence out of context. Again grammar is ready to hand to provide the required refinement of the raw lexical material:

> farmer *will kill* duckling
> farmer *must kill* duckling
> farmer *will have killed* duckling
> farmer *must have killed* duckling, *etc.*

Devices are available too for giving variable prominence to one or other of the participants in the process to identify it as the topic. We noted earlier how word order can signal an assignment of participant role (agent, patient, and so on). It can also be used to indicate what is to be presented by the speaker as the topic. But then to avoid confusion we need some way of marking the participant role distinction. In English the word *by* is used for this purpose:

hunter kill lion (hunter topic and agent, lion patient)
hunter kill by lion (hunter topic and patient, lion agent)

Add tense and aspect specifications in the correct combinations and we get:

hunter killed lion
hunter killed by lion
hunter was killing lion
hunter was killed by lion, *etc.*

The expressions we have arrived at so far still need further refinement before they are presentable as sentences of standard English. But they are gradually coming into grammatical focus. And perhaps they suffice to demonstrate, in a rudimentary way, how the arrangements and alterations of grammar provide additional specification to lexical associations so that the words can relate more precisely to features of context, including those features which are incorporated into the knowledge of the language users themselves. The greater the contribution of context in the sense of shared knowledge and experience the less need there is for grammar to augment the association of words. The less effective the words are in identifying relevant features of context in that sense, the more dependent they become on grammatical modification of one sort or another. And of course where there can be no possibility of shared contextual knowledge, as in the case of unpredictable personal invention and interpretation, grammar provides the guarantee of individual conceptual freedom. Contrary to what Tony Lumpkin believes, speaking for all those who have been subjected to the drudgery of learning it in school, grammar is not a constraining imposition but a liberating force: it frees us from a dependency on context and the limitations of a purely lexical categorization of reality.

The relationship between grammar and lexis

Grammar, then, can be seen as a resource for the adaptation of lexis. But there is no absolute distinction between the two, only a convenient distribution of semantic responsibility. Grammar is a device for indicating the most common and recurrent aspects of meaning which it would be tedious and inefficient to incorporate into separate lexical items. Thus it might be possible to have quite separate words for, say, *kills, killed, is killing*, and so on, just as we have in English separate words for *man* (male human) and *woman* (female human) or *people* (humans in the plural). But then we would have to find separate words for every action or event denoted by different lexical verbs: a mammoth and unnecessary task. So grammar simply formalizes the most widely applicable concepts, the highest common factors of experience: it provides for communicative economy. Of course, as the examples of *man, woman*, and *people* illustrate, one can economize in the opposite direction as it were, from grammar to lexis. Thus, in English, the grammatical structure *the man who brings the post* can be lexically realized as *postman; an animal which has been killed for consumption* becomes *meat*. In this respect, the dictionary and the descriptive grammar are complementary. The dictionary shows how efficiency in the formulation of meaning can be achieved by *synthesis*, the grammar shows how it can be achieved by *analysis*. Each mutually supports the other one as a compendium of conceptual and communicative resource. Together they contribute the cultural means whereby a society organizes and acts upon its environment by the establishment of communal categories of context. Such categories naturally facilitate interaction *within* linguistic communities and inhibit interaction *between* communities to the extent that they differ in their conceptual and communicative economies. These differences might have to do with the aspects of context which are differentiated and generalized, or with the distribution of responsibility for denoting these aspects within the formal resources of the language, within its lexis, morphology, and syntax.

The general issue arising here concerns the way in which lexis and grammar act upon each other in the determination of meaning. The traditional view in both linguistics and language teaching is that grammar acts upon lexis. Thus, in the case being considered here, syntax compensates for the imprecision of

simple word association by setting tense and aspect co-ordinates,
assigning subject and object roles, and so on, thereby narrowing
down contextual possibilities. It is because grammar has the
effect of refining the relatively raw conceptual material of lexis
by systematizing it in this way that it is considered as the primary
determinant. Hence the customary practice of establishing
structures and paradigms and then fitting words into them. But
we need to note that lexis can also act upon grammar. Consider,
for example, the case of the grammatical category of progressive
aspect. We are told (in Quirk *et al.* 1972: 93) that this indicates a
number of meanings, as for example:

Temporariness: activity at a particular moment, *e.g.* Joan is
singing well.
Limited duration: *e.g.* The professor is typing his own letters
(these days).
Characteristic activity: necessarily occurring with adverbs like
always and *continually*. It imparts a subjective, emotionally
coloured tone, *e.g.* John's always coming late.

Now so long as one is careful in the selection of lexical
realization, then it is possible to distinguish the different
meanings supposedly signalled by the verb form. So, for
example, an expression like *Joan is singing well* could be
understood in either the temporariness or the limited duration
sense. But this is not the case with, for example, *Joan is getting
dressed* or *John is having a shave*. These lexical items act upon
the grammar to constrain the temporariness sense since as lexical
items they denote temporary activities. *The professor is writing a
letter* suggests a temporary activity, whereas *The professor is
writing a book* suggests an activity of extended duration. But the
only difference between these two sentences lies in the choice of
the lexical item as object. And then there are cases which do not
seem to correspond with any of the given meanings. For
example:

Joan is going grey.
John is growing old.

These 'activities' are not temporary (more's the pity) but they
can hardly be equated with the professor's letter typing, which is
a periodic state of affairs and will not last. Nor is it appropriate
to call them 'characteristic activities'. Going grey and growing

old are indeed processes rather than activities, irreversible and permanent. We might compare:

The professor is typing his own letters for the time being.
*Joan is growing old for the time being.

If we use the criterion invoked for the characteristic activity sense of the progressive, namely that the admissability of an adverb signals a different sense, then we would have to increase the subcategories of meaning associated with this particular aspectual form of the verb. But then where do we stop? For it is easy to think of other examples where the lexical choice will lead to a further proliferation of senses. We have to conclude, I think, that there is a very wide range of meanings which the progressive can be associated with but that these are determined by the particular choice of lexis and are not independently a property of the grammatical category of aspect. The lexis, in this respect, acts upon the grammar.

There is, then, a reciprocal relationship between grammar and lexis: they act in concert in the discharge of their semantic duties. But we should notice that there is really no hard and fast semantic distinction between them, but only degrees of conceptual generality. Although it is common practice to distinguish what Henry Sweet called 'form-words' as distinct from 'full words' and to locate the former in grammer rather than lexis, it has to be noted that these 'form-words' have emerged over time from full-blown lexical sources, and for the most part still have recognizable kin which show clear signs of the relationship. So it is, for example, that the auxiliaries *have* and *be* co-exist with verbs of the same form which denote possession and existence and from which they derived. Similarly *do* occurs as a lexical verb but also as a purely grammatical element whose function is to carry tense and negation for the lexical verb. Compare, for example:

Joan did her homework.
Joan did not do her homework.

The scale across which this gradual historical shift takes place, a scale of increasing conceptual generality from lexical to grammatical meaning, is evident too in the current state of the language. We see lexical items of a high degree of generality which have functions which are difficult to differentiate from those of grammatical elements. Consider the following example:

John has bought one of those new micro-computers. I don't
know where we are going to put *the thing*/I don't know where
we are going to put *it*.

Thing is a lexical item, *it* is a grammatical 'function' word, but
they are hardly to be distinguished in terms of degree of
generality.

There is, then, nothing contrary to the normal operation of
language in the proposition that lexical items of high generality
like *then* and *now* should be given grammatical status as in the
examples given earlier. This process has, after all, already taken
place in the signalling of future time with *will*. We might propose
the following paradigm:

The farmer then kill duckling—*past time*
The farmer now kill duckling—*present time*
The farmer will kill duckling—*future time*

It happens that only the last of these verb phrases is standard
English. But it is easy to imagine the development of the other
two in derived or dialetical variants. One can indeed see in
pidginized forms based on English this kind of assignment of
grammatical function to lexical items of high conceptual
generality. In Cameroon pidgin, for example, *josnau* (a deriva-
tive from 'just now') is a marker of the present progressive and
nau nau a marker of the present perfect denoting the immediate
past as in:

Josnau a di chop—I am eating at the moment
A dong chop nau nau—I have only just eaten (*Todd 1974: 18*)

Similarly, in Melanesian pidgin, the grammatical function of
possession is signalled by a derived form from the lexical item
belong as in:

ples bilong mi—my place

Another point that might be made about the relationship
between the 'form-words' of grammar and the 'full words' of
lexis is that it follows from the kind of auxiliary, context-
complementary function of grammar being proposed here that
the proportional occurrence of these words will vary in different
kinds of discourse.

If, for example, language is used to *establish* a context of
shared knowledge rather than to *identify* aspects of a pre-

existing one, then there is likely to be a higher degree of explicit lexical reference and so a higher proportion of full words. The 'lexical density' of such texts will be relatively high (for a full discussion see Stubbs 1986b). Since a good deal of writing is context-establishing in this way, it generally reveals higher levels of lexical density than does, for example, spoken conversation, which tends to be context-identifying, concerned with giving the sharper indexical focus to shared lexical information which form-words can provide. But one cannot simply associate high lexical density with writing, and low lexical density with speaking. What is at issue is the way different uses of language realize the complementary relationship between linguistic resources and contextual factors.

In view of this complementary relationship of grammar and lexis, it is not surprising to find that there are units of meaning which are intermediary between lexical words and grammatical structures, the existence of which again indicates that there is a continuum between these levels of language. Such units are sentence-like in that they are syntactically combined sequences of words but they seem to be stored in the mind ready for use as preformed unitary items, like words, already assembled for immediate access. They are, therefore, formulaic in character and although they may call for some adaptation for contextual fit they are not composed on each occasion from constituent parts. They are the result of recall and not of the composition of components by the application of syntactic rules. These units have been variously referred to as lexical phrases (Nattinger 1988), composites (Cowie 1988), and lexicalized sentence stems (Pawley and Syder 1983). Pawley and Syder provide a number of examples, among them the following:

You can't be too careful.
Are you all right?
I see what you mean.
It just goes to show.
That's easier said than done.
I don't know and I don't care.
It's easy to talk.
I thought better of it.
It doesn't bear thinking about.
Think twice before you do that.
I thought you'd never ask.
Think nothing of it.

As Pawley and Syder point out, the number of such formulaic or composite expressions runs into very many thousands and the ability to apply them in use accounts for the fluency of the native speaker. They are, therefore, a crucial component of competence and they pose problems in both the description and the pedagogy of language.

With regard to description, computer analysis of text provides the means for identifying these expressions since their normality is a function of their occurrence as holistic units. So it becomes a relatively straightforward matter to list them as an inventory. But it is less easy to see how they might be described in reference to grammar on the one hand and lexis on the other. They vary in their tolerance of adjustment: some are quite flexible and some can be adjusted quite radically and these we may think of as more grammatical. Others are more fixed and allow little room for adjustment, and these we might think of as more lexical in character. But they are ranged on a continuum and a satisfactory account really depends on a theory of language which encompasses both grammar and lexis within the same descriptive scheme and makes explicit the relationship between them. At present they tend to be treated apart, so that these formulaic lexico-grammatical units are left rather in limbo.

Semantics and pragmatics

I have suggested that it is the function of grammar to reduce the range of meaning signalled by words so as to make them more effective in the identification of features of context, thereby providing for the increased indexical potential of lexis. But of course grammatical modification cannot account for the particulars of meaning which are signalled on particular occasions. Grammar can only *denote* degrees of generality. It cannot *refer* to individual cases. Now, as will have been noticed, in all the examples I have given, one very crucial element has been missing to make the expressions grammatical as instances of standard English—we need determiners of some sort. For example:

The farmer kills *a* duckling.
A hunter killed *the* lion.

And so we arrive at last at the fully focused sentence. These articles, definite and indefinite, now increase the specificity of the lexical meaning of the nouns. *The* farmer, for example, narrows attention to one who is known to both speaker and hearer, *a* farmer indicates one who is not. But the hearer still has to act on this indication and find which particular farmer is thereby being referred to. All the grammar does is to signal that there is one. As with the other grammatical devices we have been considering, the function of the article is to set contextual co-ordinates in a way which narrows down the range of inference.

We come here to the question of the relationship between lexis/grammar on the one hand and context on the other, between semantics and pragmatics. This is explored further in Chapter 7, but we might note in passing here that the extent to which these contextual co-ordinates are encoded within grammar varies across languages: what is semantically signalled by grammatical means in one language is left for pragmatic inference in another. To the extent that the grammar formalizes the same principles as those of preferred pragmatic inference one can think of grammar, as Levinson has suggested, as 'frozen pragmatics' (Levinson 1987). Such a suggestion is, of course, entirely consistent with the ideas about the function of grammar as outlined in this chapter.

To illustrate this distribution of work between semantic encoding and pragmatic inference, that is to say, the extent to which grammar fixes the contextual co-ordinates, consider the following English expressions:

1 The president wanted to resign.
2 The president wanted him to resign.
3 The president said he wanted to resign.
4 The president assumed he wanted to resign.

In sentence 1 the identity of the person who wants to resign is grammatically established as the president and in sentence 2 it is established as some male person who is *not* the president: the grammar itself specifies disjunctive reference for *him*. In sentences 3 and 4, the reference value of *he* may be either the president or some other male person. Although one would probably incline pragmatically to the former interpretation in sentence 3 and to the latter interpretation in sentence 4, the context could easily override these preferences—most obviously, perhaps, in the case of the president being a woman. On the other hand, sentences 1 and 2 are impervious to such contextual effects. But of course, even here there is pragmatic work to do to establish the identity of the people concerned. The use of definite reference and third person pronoun signal that shared knowledge is to be engaged, that is to say, that contextual information is needed which is not abstracted in the codified forms of grammar. In all these cases, what needs to be inferred is the relationship between what has become generally conceptualized in grammatical form and what is particular in context.

Communication, then, can only be achieved by relating language with context: grammar simply makes it easier to establish the relationship by setting, as it were, more exact co-ordinates. But the language user is still left with the problem of engaging the particular features of actuality which are relevant on a specific occasion. Knowing these devices for narrowing down contextual possibilities does not imply that one can judge how best to act upon such knowledge, how much can be left to be inferred from context, how much needs to be made grammatically explicit. Something must always be left unsaid. But how much? An example from history might serve to illustrate the point: another instance of the possible disasters attendant on an ineffective use of grammar.

The scene is the Battle of Balaclava. On high ground, at a customary safe distance from the action, the British general Lord Raglan is directing troop movements by sending his orders by messengers on horseback. From his vantage point he sees in one part of the field the enemy trying to retreat with their artillery and he sends a message to his brigade of light Cavalry. It reads as follows:

> 'Lord Raglan wishes the Cavalry to advance rapidly to the front, follow the enemy and try to prevent the enemy carrying away the guns.'

The Cavalry commanders, Lord Cardigan and Lord Lucan, receiving this message, recognize that the definite articles signal a particular front of battle and particular guns which both they and Lord Raglan are supposed to know about. But they are in the valley. Lord Raglan is upon the heights. The commanders cannot actually see what Lord Raglan intends to refer to. They do not in fact share the same context. The general has made an unwarranted assumption about shared knowledge. The only front that the Cavalry commanders can see is right at the end of the valley where the main Russian army is massively assembled, secure behind their heavy guns. For them *this* front and *these* guns are the only possible ones indicated by the definite articles. So, since theirs is not to reason why, they attack, with disastrous consequences. And that is how the Charge of the Light Brigade, the most celebrated and glorious calamity in British military history came about—all because of a failure in the effective use of grammar to make an appropriate connection with context. Not all such failures, of course, are as historically momentous. But they are of very common occurrence.

Grammar and learning

But let us return to Tony Lumpkin once more: 'Grammar, and nonsense, and learning'. What about learning? I have presented grammar as a device for mediating between words and contexts. The device itself is very complex, and its complexity cannot be explained only by invoking communicative function (see Newmeyer 1983). It is subject to other informing influences: the general and essential parameters of universal grammar; the particular and accidental developments of its own social history. But for language learners to learn only the intricacies of the device without knowing how to put it to use is rather like learning about the delicate mechanisms of a clock without knowing how to tell the time. What is crucial for learners to know is how grammar functions in alliance with words and contexts for the achievement of meaning.

The teaching of grammar, as traditionally practised, does not promote such an alliance. On the contrary, it is the formal properties of the device which are commonly given prominence. Words come in only as convenient for purposes of illustration. In other words, lexis is put to the service of grammar. But as I have shown, the function of grammar depends upon its being subservient to lexis. Teaching which gives primacy to form and uses words simply as a means of exemplification actually denies the nature of grammar as a construct for the mediation of meaning. I would suggest that a more natural and more effective approach would be to reverse this traditional pedagogic dependency, begin with lexical items and show how they need to be grammatically modified to be communicatively effective.

Within the category of lexical items, I include the formulaic patterns I referred to earlier. If they do figure so prominently in competence, it does not seem reasonable just to disregard their existence and leave their learning to chance. Studies in first language (see Peters 1983) and second language acquisition (see Gleason 1982; Vihman 1982) suggest that the way learners proceed is to begin with these units as lexical complexes associated with certain contexts and then pick them apart analytically as the need arises. Some are dismantled entirely into separate components for generative reassembly in reference to grammatical rule, others are partly dismantled but are left as adaptable formulaic frameworks to be adjusted to circumstances; some again remain as holistically fixed, essentially large-scale lexical items.

In view of this one might consider presenting language as lexical units, both as single words and as complex packages, and then creating contexts which constrain the gradual elaboration of the first, the gradual analysis of the second. In this way grammar would not be presented as primary but as a consequence of the achievement of meaning through the modification of lexical items. This would not imply that all of the many thousands of formulaic expressions would be expressly taught. The object would be to use them to develop learning procedures which would provide the basis for learners subsequently to process language and acquire the packaged units for themselves.

Such an approach to language presentation of course means that contexts have to be contrived to motivate this lexical modification and to guide the learner in the discriminating and differential use of grammatical analysis. Again, traditional teaching has tended to dissociate grammar from context and to deal in isolated sentences. A pedagogy which aimed at teaching the functional potential of grammar along the lines I have described, would have to get learners to engage in problem-solving tasks which required a gradual elaboration of grammar to service an increasing precision in the identification of relevant features of context. In this way, learners would realize the communicative value of grammar in the very achievement of meaning.

I use the term 'realize' here in a deliberate double sense. On the one hand the approach I am proposing would lead the learners to realize (in the sense of *actualize*) grammatical potential in contexts of use, that is to say that it would lead to effective behaviour. But on the other hand, the approach would also make learners realize (in the sense of *recognize*) the significance of grammar, and raise their consciousness of its relevance.

A distinction is commonly made between teaching language and teaching about language and the belief is expressed that the first has to be done by providing direct experience and avoiding the explicit knowledge promoted by the second. Conscious awareness and reflection on one's own experience is thought to have an inhibiting effect. A version of this belief is incorporated into Krashen's distinction between (unconscious) acquisition and (conscious) learning, already discussed in Chapter 2. Now although there will obviously be occasions when this belief is warranted, when learners are of an age, for example, at which they would not have the capacity or disposition for analytic self-reflection, there seems no good reason for supposing that the belief is universally valid. On the contrary it seems on the face of it to be likely that with some learners a conscious awareness of how language works and the subjection of their experience to analysis would suit their cognitive style, increase motivation by giving added point to their activities, and so enhance learning. It would enable them to make comparisons between the language they are learning and their own language, and engage in the kind of rational enquiry which is encouraged in other subjects on the curriculum. In this way the language to be learned could be associated with a wider experience of language and education. There are, then, arguments in favour of such consciousness-raising (see also Sharwood-Smith 1981; Rutherford 1987). The question, as always, is how they apply in particular cases.

It seems sometimes to be supposed that what is commendable about a communicative approach to language teaching is that it does not, as a structural approach does, have to get learners to puzzle their heads with grammar. If we are looking for nonsense, this suggestion is a prime example. For if this were really the case, a communicative approach would have little or nothing to commend it. For language learning *is* essentially learning how grammar functions in the achievement of meaning and it is a mistake to suppose otherwise. The question is how should grammar be learned so that its intrinsic communicative character is understood and acted upon. This cannot be done by restricting attention to its formal properties, the relations and regularities which make up the internal mechanism of the device. No matter how legitimate it might be to define the scope of linguistics in this way (and this is currently a controversial matter), it will not do for language pedagogy. Learners need to realize the *function* of the device as a way of mediating between words and contexts, as a powerful resource for the purposeful achievement of meaning. A communicative approach, properly conceived, does not involve the rejection of grammar. On the contrary, it involves a recognition of its central mediating role in the use and learning of language.

7 The Negotiation of meaning

Sentence meaning and utterance meaning

Grammar, as I pointed out in the preceding chapter, can only go so far. When it has done its work there still remains the task of relating it to aspects of the context which are particular and cannot of their nature be accounted for in advance. In this chapter I shall consider in more detail what is involved in this task, how context acts upon grammar so that the specific meanings of particular expressions are realized and communicative outcomes brought about. So we move from semantics to pragmatics, from virtual to actual meaning.

What I am seeking to do is to outline a model of language use. But we must also bear in mind, particularly in view of the points raised in Chapter 5, that such a model needs to be evaluated in terms of its pedagogic relevance. How far is such a model serviceable for language learning? How far is it congruent, or in competition with, the model of grammar outlined in the last chapter? But before these questions are addressed we need to consider the model of how meanings are realized in context.

We can begin with the crucial, if rather obvious, point that understanding what people mean by what they say is not the same as understanding the linguistic expressions they use in saying it. This is simple enough to demonstrate. Consider an expression in English. The following will do:

The letter is in the drawer.

Considered as a sentence this poses no problem for understanding. But as a *use* of language, as an utterance, presented like this in isolation, it is quite incomprehensible, because we cannot attach any meaning to it. The idiom is significant: we attach meanings to linguistic expressions, and we do this by invoking some pre-existing knowledge or other, or some co-existing feature of the situation of utterance. Anybody actually producing this expression with the intention of being meaningful would suppose that the addressee can make an attachment, can relate the language to some shared conception or perception of the world and so *achieve* the intended meaning. *The letter* (the one we have just been talking about, the one that arrived by post this morning, the one containing Aunt Kitty's cheque . . .) *is in the drawer* (the one in the desk, the one in the dressing table upstairs, the one in the kitchen where we always put the post . . .). Every linguistic expression contains the potential for a multiplicity of meanings and which one is realized on a particular occasion is determined by non-linguistic factors of context.

A sentence has only one invariant meaning, or if it has more than one, as in the case of structural or lexical ambiguity, its meanings can be exactly specified. Utterances, on the other hand, are protean in character. Their meanings change continually to suit the circumstances in which they are used.

We must be careful, however, not to be too carried away by this idea. The multiplicity of utterance meanings does not mean that any linguistic expression can mean anything at all in complete disregard of what it means as a sentence. I cannot say that the letter is in the drawer and mean that the cake is in the cupboard, or that the letter *was* or *will be* in the drawer. The conventional meaning of linguistic signs, and their combinations in sentences, constitutes *types* of conceptualization codified as linguistic knowledge and the *tokens* of particular and actualized instances must clearly be set in correspondence with them. The letter I am referring to now at the moment is a particular token instance of *letter* as a lexical item, a general conceptual type, a codified abstraction. It is simply that the type is more or less stable, established by convention, whereas the token is not since it is conditioned by context. And language use must always be a matter of actualizing tokens as appropriate.

I say 'more or less stable' because, of course, conventions of meaning change over time. Hence the need to revise dictionaries and grammars as certain particularities of use become general-ized as usage. And these conventions are not of common currency throughout a speech community. A dictionary, for example, does not record meanings which are within the competence of all language users. As Johnson-Laird has pointed out we customarily understand and use words in context whose meanings we do not know in any exact sense:

Discourse rarely depends upon speakers having complete and identical representations of the meanings of the words they use. It is perfectly possible to communicate with little or no such similarity or else children would never learn their native tongue. Adults, too, can communicate successfully with an incomplete knowledge of meaning. When, for example, you read the sentence:

After a hearty dish of spaghetti, Bernini cast a bronze of a mastiff searching for truffles.

you may understand it perfectly well even though, on reflection, you may not be entirely sure exactly what alloy *bronze* is, or what sort of dog a *mastiff* is, or what *truffles* are." *(1983: 225)*

So the type of meaning that is known may be very general (*bronze* is a kind of metal, *mastiff* a kind of dog). All that is required is that it can be realized as a token which is sufficient for the purpose of the communication concerned. There will, of course, be occasions when the purpose calls for increased specificity of type: we would need to be more knowledgeable about the precise meaning of *bronze*, for example, in the context of a textbook on metallurgy. But then the argument would apply to other words in that context which had less bearing on the purpose in reading.

Communication, then, is a matter of the mutual accommodation of type and token as appropriate to purpose. Our concepts of meaning provide us with bearings on what words mean in context and the context in turn provides us with evidence for extending our conceptual representation of these meanings.

Symbol and index

It will be convenient to mark the distinctions I have been drawing by means of certain semiotic terms. I introduced them briefly in Chapter 6 and it is now time to consider them more closely. The linguistic sign as type we can call the *symbol*. A knowledge of language will enable us to decipher strings of symbols as sentences and it is this knowledge, generally referred to as linguistic competence, which it is the traditional business of linguists to account for, and the traditional business of language teachers to teach. Comprehension in the sense of understanding sentences is then a semantic matter of deciphering symbolic meanings. But this knowledge will not alone enable us to understand language in use for this is always a matter of realizing the particular token meanings of signs in association with the context of utterance. This is a pragmatic matter of achieving meaning by using linguistic signs as evidence. The sign in the utterance, therefore, does not function as a symbol but as an *index*: it indicates where we must look in the world we know or can perceive in order to discover meaning. It directs our attention away from the language itself. In the case of the letter and the drawer, the signs fail in their indexical function because, appearing as they do in an isolated expression, they simply direct us into a void. They can be deciphered semantically as symbols without difficulty, but they cannot be interpreted pragmatically as indices (for further discussion see Widdowson 1983, 1984a: Paper 9).

Whereas symbolic meanings inhere in the signs themselves, indexical meanings must be achieved by the language user associating symbols with some relevant aspect of the world outside language, in the situation or in the mind. This association may be fairly straightforward, the range of possible reference fairly narrow, and then the interpretation of what the addresser intends is easy. People who have particular knowledge and experience in common, whose contextual realities, so to speak, are closely congruent, will manage to communicate by engaging relevant aspects of contexts with only sparing use of the linguistic resources at their disposal. Conversely, of course, those who have little in common have to place greater reliance on the language.

But we do not only communicate with people with whom we share our personal lives. We need also to participate in wider networks of interaction which extend from the individual into a complexity of connections with the groups and institutions that constitute the society we live in. And here we cannot rely on particular instances of shared knowledge and experience. We need to refer to more general and conventional assumptions and beliefs which define what is accepted as normal or typical in respect of the way reality is structured and to the conduct of social life. This common knowledge of shared experience and conventionally sanctioned reality can be called *schematic* knowledge: it is the knowledge which is acquired as a condition of entry into a particular culture or sub-culture.

Schematic knowledge, then, is a necessary source of reference in use whereby linguistic symbols are converted into indices in the process of interpretation. But we should note, too, that language development itself, the acquisition of knowledge of symbolic meanings, is activated by the need to extend schematic knowledge so as to cope more effectively with the social environment. We learn language in order to manage our affairs in the world we find ourselves in. Language is the means of initiation into the conventions of conceptualization and communication which define particular cultures. It has a crucial socializing purpose. Formal education extends this process by providing guidance into different ways of conceiving of the world and different ways of conveying these concepts in modes of description, argument, and so on. Particular subjects on the curriculum can be seen as different sub-cultures in which reality is variously reformulated.

But if it is the case that language learning is activated by the socio-cultural purpose of schematic extension, that we learn language in order to get a better grasp of the world so that we can turn it to our advantage, then it would seem to follow that a central problem in the teaching of a foreign language lies in the provision of some comparable activating purpose. In other words, we need to identify areas of schematic knowledge which the learners will accept as independently relevant and worth acquiring so that the learning of the language is seen as the necessary means to a desired end. If this is so, the first question to be asked in designing a language course should not be 'What language do we need to teach?' but rather 'What do we need to teach that will stimulate the learning of language?' The defining of the subject English is in this view primarily not a matter of language but of non-linguistic content. One might argue then that the effectiveness of language teaching will depend on what is being taught, other than the language, that will be recognized by the learners as a purposeful and relevant extension of their schematic horizons.

This argument can be invoked to support the programme of language immersion in Canada, referred to in Chapter 2, and other proposals to associate the foreign language more closely with other subjects on the curriculum (see, for example, Widdowson 1968, 1978). The idea of task-based learning in general also bears on this issue. The success of such tasks as activators of language use for learning will depend on the extent to which they engage the learner in conceptual and communicative activities which they feel are worthwhile in their own right (see Prabhu 1987).

There are matters concerning the teaching of languages for specific purposes (LSP) which come up for consideration here as well. It would seem by its very name that this enterprise is indeed concerned with associating language with purpose. But the purpose has not always been taken as primary in the pedagogic approach adopted. Often specific language associated with the eventual purpose has been identified and then activities devised which lead to no schematic extension, either because the specialist content is familiar or because the tasks are not designed to engage appropriate modes of thinking. Hence although the language is related to purpose this is not realized in the process of learning (for further discussion see Widdowson 1983: Chapter 3).

We may say, then, that the achievement of indexical meaning is commonly a matter of making a connection between the linguistic sign and the relevant aspect of schematic knowledge. If we refer to linguistic knowledge, the internalization of the symbolic function of signs, *systemic* knowledge, then we can think of the realization of meaning in actual language use as a matter of taking bearings on two points of reference: systemic knowledge on the one hand and schematic knowledge on the other.

Now, one can distinguish two kinds of schematic knowledge. On the one hand there is knowledge of conceptual content or topic area. This I have referred to elsewhere as 'ideational' (Widdowson 1983). Carrell (1983, 1987), who has been much occupied in determining the effects of schematic knowledge on reading comprehension, refers to such knowledge constructs as 'content schemata'. These she defines as 'background knowledge about the content area of a text—for example, a text about washing clothes, celebrating New Year's Eve in Hawaii, building a canoe, or about the economy of Mexico, the history of Canada, problems of nuclear breeder reactors, etc.' (Carrell 1983: 84). The other kind of schematic knowledge has to do with mode of communication. This I have referred to elsewhere as 'interpersonal' (Widdowson 1983). Carrell's term for it is 'formal' and she defines it as 'background knowledge about the formal, rhetorical, organizational structures of different kinds of texts' (1983: 83–4).

Negotiating procedures

This taking of bearings on systemic and schematic knowledge is the procedural activity which converts type to token, symbol to index, and so actualizes particular meanings. It is the continuous process of plotting a position and steering an interpretative course by adjustment and prediction. It is in this sense that language use can be regarded as essentially a matter of the negotiation of meaning.

It will be clear that on any particular occasion of meaning negotiation the more familiar the schematic content or mode of communication, the less reliance needs to be placed on systemic knowledge, and vice versa. If, for example, I am engaged in reading a text on a subject in which I am well versed (where the ideational or content schema is familiar), which has been written in a manner conventionally associated with writing on this subject (where the interpersonal or formal schema is familiar), then I shall only need to pay attention to the linguistic signs to the extent that they key in this schematic knowledge and indicate how it is to be extended. Many of the specific meanings which can be deciphered out of the symbol are not activated because they are not indexically required. This, of course, relates to the point made by Johnson-Laird earlier: that an effective (i.e. indexical) use of language does not depend on knowing precise (i.e. symbolically complete) meanings.

On the other hand, if I encounter a text which deals with an unfamiliar content area and does so in accordance with communicative or rhetorical conventions which are new to me, then I obviously have to look much more closely at the language itself as a source of information as to what might be meant. I have to count on the symbol itself as providing the main evidence for meaning and, of course, as providing the means for creating schematic knowledge which I do not have in advance. In brief, if schematic knowledge is in short supply on a particular occasion, then the more we need to invoke systemic knowledge as a means of compensating for the deficiency and if we are thereby able to convert symbol to index, then the act of meaning negotiation itself has the effect of extending or altering the schematic knowledge we started with. This is the process we call learning.

As an illustration of this learning process, consider the following passage:

Oil-bound paints may sometimes fail when used on certain building materials. When an acid and alkali react together the result is a salt and water. If the acid is fatty such as linseed oil, then the result is a soap and water. This is known as saponification. Many building materials such as lime mortars and plasters, Portland cement and asbestos cement develop alkalis. If such surfaces are coated with an oil-bound paint, particularly in the presence of even small quantities of moisture, they will cause saponification. The paint may blister in a mild attack or show yellow soapy runs in a severe attack.

If one is already in possession of schematic (content) know-ledge about oil-bound paints and building materials, then one will already know that the former contains acids like the fatty acid in linseed oil and the other contains alkalis, that soap contains salt, and so on. Interpretation of the passage is thereby facilitated and one can use it selectively to pick up additional information to extend the schema—that the reaction referred to is known as saponification, for example. But without such knowledge, the reader is required to focus on the language and make considerable efforts of inference. Thus one has to infer that the second statement here functions as some kind of explanation of the first statement in the passage, so that the failure of oil-bound paints on certain building materials is caused by the reaction of an acid and an alkali. So acids, it would seem, are associated with the paints, alkalis with the building materials. This is confirmed later when examples of these 'certain' building materials are provided (lime mortars and plasters, etc.). The relationship between the second and third statement is problem-atic for the unknowledgeable reader. At first sight it would seem that there are two possible results from acid + alkali reaction. Closer consideration, however, reveals that this cannot be the case. 'When an acid and alkali react together' means when (all) acids and (all) alkalis react together: the structure here signals a general statement. It follows that the next statement, which provides a particular instance of the general category (*the* acid . . . such as linseed oil), must be an illustration, so a soap is a particular manifestation of a salt, and saponification a particular example of the general process of acid + alkali reaction.

So it is that close attention to the language itself and reference to systemic knowledge allows us to negotiate meaning and acquire the kind of information which for the reader in the schematic know is provided in advance.

If one's purpose is to develop the ability to negotiate meaning in this way, then one would choose to present students with passages whose content was unfamiliar. But it would be necessary to ensure that the learning which resulted in respect of such content was accepted by students as worth the processing effort. In the present case, one would suppose that information about the effect of paint on building materials is of fairly limited appeal.

Reciprocal and non-reciprocal negotiation

Of course, if occasions arise when the symbols resist indexical conversion, for all our procedural efforts, then interpretation will fail. In this case, the addresser, the message sender, has made unwarranted assumptions about the extent to which the same schematic knowledge is shared by the receiver, and leaves too many gaps, or gaps too broad to be bridged. When this happens in reciprocal discourse, in face to face conversation, where the discourse develops by the exchange of speaker role, then the situation can be remedied (given the impulse to co-operate and to accommodate the reality of the interlocutor's world) by an overtly interactive negotiation whereby intention and interpreta-tion are brought into an approximate convergence as required by the purpose of the interaction. Two people who speak the same language can always work towards an understanding about what each of them is talking about and what each of them wishes to achieve by what they say. They can therefore make their meanings *accessible* by talk. Of course, they may not *accept* the beliefs, attitudes, or intentions that are expressed; one can always object to what somebody else says, but it does not make much sense to do this unless one understands its meaning.

In reciprocal discourse, then, interlocutors can always estab-lish, by the turn-taking of talk, the necessary grounds of shared knowledge, and so arrive at a mutually satisfactory schematic convergence. But the case is different of course in modes of language use which are non-reciprocal, of which what I am doing at this moment is an obvious example. As I write, I make assumptions about what my reader already knows about language and language learning, about the common ground of knowledge, and what he or she cannot be expected to know since it concerns the idiosyncrasies of my own view of these matters. So I have to make decisions as I go along as to which points need to be spelled out, which of them can be stated sparely, or which of them do not need to be mentioned at all but can be left to be inferred. No negotiation by active and reciprocal participation is possible: the reader and writer cannot, as conversationalists can, work together in directing the course of the communication. This does not mean that no negotiation takes place. The writer is engaged in a kind of vicarious interaction with a presumed reader and anticipates and provides for likely reactions. The reader for his part is drawn into the discourse role that the writer has cast him in (for further discussion see Widdowson 1979: Paper 13; 1984a: Section 2).

But of course the writer's assumptions may be mistaken: the reader may know more or less than has been assumed, in which case the negotiation will falter. If the reader has more knowledge than the writer has supposed, then he will tend to disregard the discourse that has been plotted in the act of writing and simply take from the text whatever best suits his purpose. If the reader knows less of the writer's world than supposed, he will have to draw on systemic knowledge to furnish the necessary clues and if this strategy fails, then the meanings remain inaccessible, the text non-negotiable.

I have talked of the negotiation of meaning as a function of the *convergence* of schematic knowledge, achieved by the *conversion* of symbol to index. But it should be noted that this convergence need not be complete. It is unlikely that we ever achieve an exact match between intention and interpretation, and we probably would not know it if we did. We arrive at the degree of convergence necessary to the purpose of interaction and no more. Comprehension is never complete: it is always only approximate, and relative to purpose.

So far in this chapter I have focused on meaning negotiation as a matter of *transaction*. But we need to recognize its *interactional* character as well (see Brown and Yule 1983). I mentioned earlier that a particular meaning might be made accessible but that it does not necessarily follow that it will be acceptable. The effective transaction of communicative business requires the parties concerned to enter into a sort of social contract involving adherence to what has been called the 'Co-operative Principle' (see Grice 1975). Language cannot symbolically signal its own meaning but has to be contextually connected to yield indexical meaning, so it follows that some mutually agreed ground rules for co-operation have to be assumed. We suppose, for instance, that what somebody says to us will be relevant to the occasion or to what has just been said, that people do not just issue utterances at random. We suppose that when somebody says something to us, it is meant to be informative, has some warrant in fact and is not a deliberate obfuscation or falsehood (for further detail and discussion see Grice 1975; Levinson 1983; Sperber and Wilson 1986).

Now if these maxims of co-operation are not honoured by a speaker on a particular occasion and the hearer has reason to suppose that this is intentional, the hearer will look for meanings other than those which are explicitly expressed. If it is obvious to both of them that what the speaker has just said is false, or so obvious as to need no comment at all, the hearer will look for *implications*, that is to say what is implied other than what is expressed.

But why should these maxims be flouted in this way? Why should people deny the co-operative principle by being deviant, making their meanings less accessible, their transactions therefore less effective?

The answer is that there is an affective as well as effective consideration in the negotiation of meaning. To communicate we need to co-operate. But co-operation involves risks. It requires us to move into somebody else's territory of self and to leave our own vulnerable to intrusion. We therefore tend to be circumspect and protective, particularly of course when our dealings involve some threat to the fragile security of the other person's composure or self-esteem, or our own (for further discussion see Brown and Levinson 1978; Widdowson 1984a: Paper 7). The negotiation of meaning which is both accessible and acceptable, therefore, involves the reconciliation of two potentially opposing forces: the co-operative imperative which acts in the interests of the effective conveyance of messages, and the territorial imperative which acts in the interests of the affective wellbeing of self. One imperative might impel the speaker to be direct, to get the message across; the other might impel the speaker to be deviant, to avoid offence or embarrassment. Where reciprocal interaction is concerned in particular, the achievement of communicative purpose also involves, indeed depends upon, the maintenance of rapport between the interlocutors. Those participating in conversational encounters have to have a care for the preservation of good relations by promoting the other's positive self-image, by avoiding offence, encouraging comity, and so on. The negotiation of meaning is also a negotiation of social relations. And indeed in some cases of conversation, the maintenance of rapport, the sharing of affective territory, the achievement of mutually acceptable states of mind is not the means towards an effective communicative transaction but the very object of the interaction itself. People often talk to each other *in order to* lower their territorial barriers, to indulge in the pleasure of rapport, the sharing of common ground. There may be very little transactional business enacted, or effectively none at all (see Aston 1986).

The negotiation of meaning and language learning

So much for the general account for how (as I see it) meaning is achieved in the natural use of language. I turn now to the question of the relevance of such an account to language learning, in particular as that process is carried out in classrooms under the direction, or at least the surveillance, of the teacher.

Perhaps the first point that needs to be made is that the relationship between use and learning differs in respect to first and second language situations. In natural first language acquisition, the child, growing up through involvement in naturally recurrent events, learns about the world through language and concomitantly learns language through an engagement with the world. The two processes are, so to speak, symbiotically related; they are the mutually reinforcing determinants of development. Thus systemic and schematic knowledge develop concurrently, each supportive of the other. This experience cannot be replicated in second language acquisition. Here learners have already been socialized into the schematic knowledge associated with their mother tongue: they are initiated into their culture in the very process of language learning. When they confront uses of the foreign language they are learning, their natural inclination is to interpret them in reference to this established association, and rely on the foreign language as sparingly as possible. They will invoke as much systemic knowledge of this language as is indexically necessary and no more, using both their first language and the foreign language tactically as a source of clues to meaning, while taking bearings, as usual, on their schematic knowledge.

The nature of learner error comes up for consideration here. When learners are called upon to use the language being learned for some communicative purpose, a purpose other than language practice, then they will be naturally disposed to draw upon the systemic resources which have proved serviceable in the past for the achievement of indexical meaning. These, of course, have been predominantly those of the mother tongue. In this respect learner errors which reveal first language influence are the natural reflex of procedures of meaning negotiation.

Errors have generally been attributed to cognitive causes, evidence of the learner's psychological process of rule formation. But they can also be seen as communicatively motivated, the realization of available resources to get a message across. Thus although it may be the case that communicative demands result in error because the learner does not have enough time to access second language systemic knowledge, equally they may do so because such demands quite naturally lead learners to call upon whatever resources they have at their disposal, some of which will be drawn from their own language. It is also likely, in reference to the matters discussed in Chapter 6, that under communicative pressure learners will place more reliance on lexical means than on the intuitive assumption that context can compensate for an absence of refinement in grammatical signalling. In this respect, the errors of learners have some resemblance to other uses of language where the exigencies of the communicative situation license the disregard of grammatical niceties: telegrams, for example, or the laconic instructions of the surgeon who appeared in the preceding chapter. In short, then, errors can be referred to social/communicative as well as psychological/cognitive causes.

In view of all this, one might characterize second language pedagogy as a set of activities designed to bring about the gradual shift of reliance from one systemic resource to another for the achievement of indexical purposes.

The essential point is that meaning negotiation, which, in normal circumstances, is always a matter of achieving an objective by the most economical means, will be carried out by taking whatever short cuts are available. It does not in itself provide conditions for the acquisition of a systemic knowledge of the foreign language, in spite of what those may say who speak of 'comprehensible input' as the determining factor in the acquisition process (cf. Krashen 1982 and the discussion in

Chapter 2). The internalization of the system as a communicat-ive resource is only likely to happen when there is a concentra-ion on symbol to index conversion, when the potential value of symbols is actualized indexically in the process of discovering new meaning; that is to say, when there is a recurrent association of new schematic knowledge with new systemic knowledge. Such a state of affairs is normal in first language acquisition, where there is a concurrent discovery of language and the world, as I suggested earlier. But this focusing on form, as a condition for comprehension, will usually have to be artificially induced by some contrivance or other in a foreign language situation.

Now it might be objected that I am talking here about language knowledge and not communicative behaviour, about how grammar might be learned and not about the development of a language using ability. The point here, I think, is that if the latter is to *be* an ability, and not just a performance repertoire, then it has to be based on the internalization of systemic knowledge as a communicative resource. There is a tendency these days, and in some places, to suppose that systemic knowledge will be acquired as a natural corollary to commun-icative activities. This supposition is, I think, based on the simplistic idea that the natural conditions of language learning through use that obtain in a first language setting and in naturalistic contexts for second language acquisition can be directly replicated in foreign language classrooms.

And yet our eventual objective must be to prepare learners to cope with the natural conditions of language *use*. We come here to what seems to me to be the central dilemma in second language pedagogy: the conditions appropriate for acquiring communicative resources are different from the conditions of their use.

Consider in this connection the point I made earlier that comprehension is necessarily incomplete and dependent on purpose. Now if the intention is to elicit authentic behaviour corresponding to that of the natural language user, then learners need to be primed with purpose before they are required to give evidence of understanding, and indeed the evidence itself has to be of the kind which would emerge as a natural outcome. The reading of the passage, or the listening to an extract of spoken language, has to be such as to be dependent, a part of some activity of broader significance which provides it with a cause and a consequence which have independent point. If one rejects this authenticity condition, then one has to find ways of presenting comprehension tasks so that the learner's interest is engaged in spite of the artificiality, so that they are induced into co-operating with the contrivance. In the first case, with a dependent text, one has to allow for the exercise of schematic knowledge which will to some degree lead to the bypassing of language and the avoidance of inference. It will deflect attention from the language itself: acting as an authentic user, the learner denies himself access to the necessary data for learning. In the second case, with a detached text, more reliance will have to be placed on inference and the use of systemic knowledge. But if we seek to direct attention to this text as data to stimulate the acquisition of systemic knowledge, we run the risk of making the learner press for precision of meaning beyond any real purpose, thereby misrepresenting the very nature of language use. In the first case we have the *simulation* of user behaviour, in the second case the *stimulation* of learning behaviour. Both have their pedagogic uses but they will logically refer to different criteria for the selection of texts and the design of tasks.

The question then is, how can we continue to induce both the internalization of language as a resource and the ability to use it appropriately? I shall examine this question in more detail in the chapters in Part 3, but meanwhile we might consider briefly how different approaches to language pedagogy in general can be characterized in reference to this question.

Simplifying somewhat, we might say that a structural approach to language teaching lays emphasis on systemic knowledge and makes the assumption that once this is acquird the learners will discover for themselves how it is put to use in communication. Classroom activities will tend to be those focusing attention on deciphering rather than on interpretation by indexical inference. Language difficulty will generally be measured in terms of decipherability, the problem of which can be eased by reducing the symbolic complexity of the text.

A notional/functional approach essentially seeks to establish correlations between systemic and schematic elements. It associates concepts and communicative acts with their most common or 'standard' expressions in the foreign language. In this respect, it focuses on lexical/grammatical co-occurrences in formulaic phrases of the kind discussed in Chapter 6. Classroom activities here would prepare the learners to recognize the relevant co-occurrences and correlations as they occur in actual use. Language difficulty will be seen in terms of nonconformity to standard or normal ways of expressing notions and functions.

Neither approach takes as its central concern the exercise of procedures for meaning negotiation, which require the relating and mutual adjustment of systemic and schematic knowledge for the realization of indexical value, after the manner previously described, and which can provide the learner with the opportunity to learn the language through using it.

But an approach which did promote a negotiation of meaning in a natural way, seeking to cast the learner into the role of user, would itself run into problems, as I have indicated. For it would encourage a reliance on schematic knowledge and a corresponding avoidance of an engagement with the systemic features of the foreign language, or at best a tactical use of them which would not lead to their internalization as a more general strategic resource.

What seems to be needed is an approach which recognizes the necessary contrivance of pedagogy and seeks to guide learners through graded negotiating tasks. These would require them to take bearings on both systemic and schematic knowledge and would shift the focus of procedural work in a controlled way. There seems to be no obvious reason why such tasks should not also allow learners to refer to the systemic and schematic knowledge of their own language and culture. This would take pedagogic advantage of the learners' own experience, and would help to ensure that the tasks were independently purposeful—a crucial design feature if the tasks are to induce language processing consistent with natural use.

The purpose of such an approach would be to demonstrate that the second language has the same potential for use as the first language, encourage learners to draw on their own experience of language by applying familiar procedures to the interpretation of second language use, and so to teach the second language system not as an end in itself but as a resource for the achievement of meaning. But such an approach raises a number of issues in pedagogy about course design, methodology, and the roles of teacher and learner. These issues are taken up and considered in more detail in Part 3.

PART THREE

Aspects of teaching

8 General perspectives on pedagogy

In the preceding part of this book (Chapters 5–7), I outlined two approaches to the description of language, showed how they are related, and indicated certain implications for teaching that seemed to follow from them. In this part I want to pursue these implications in more detail, focusing on pedagogy.

The two approaches to language description can be called the semantic and the pragmatic. The semantic approach provides an account of how the language contains within itself, within its grammar and lexis, the essential resources for meaning. The pragmatic approach on the other hand focuses on how these resources have to be exploited for language users to achieve meaning. On the one hand, then, we have meaning seen in terms of a potential contained within linguistic forms. On the other hand, we have meaning seen in terms of the procedures and contextual conditions that come into play in order for this potential to be realized. These two approaches to language description are, as I have indicated, complementary. They inform different approaches to language pedagogy. These too can be seen as complementary, although they are commonly presented in opposition.

Communicative language teaching

One way of characterizing the pedagogy of language teaching in vogue over the past ten years or so is to say that it is, in a word, communicative. But this is not very illuminating. The term has been bandied about so freely, has been so liberally used as a general marker of approbation, that its descriptive value has all but vanished.

For one thing, we need to be clear whether the term is meant to refer to the *purpose* or to the *process* of learning. It is often supposed that the structural approach (what Prabhu (1987) has recently dubbed as S.O.S.—structural-oral-situational) denied the communicative purpose of language teaching and proposed in its stead that of structural manipulation. But this is not so. The emphasis on structures was associated with the *process* of learning, as the means towards an end, and this was not at all intended to preclude a communicative *purpose*. On the contrary, it was intended to promote it. This is clear from the quotation from Lado which I cited in Chapter 2 (see pages 11–12). Here structural manipulation through pattern practice is proposed as a process which facilitates a communicative purpose. Lado argues that such practice, far from confining the learner to mechanistic performance, creates conditions for effective communicative use. It leads to the internalization of patterns at a subconscious level, and thereby leaves the mind 'free to dwell on the message conveyed through the language'. These patterns, says Lado, are reduced to habit, where they belong, 'so that the mind and personality may be freed to dwell in their proper realm, that is on the meaning of the communication rather than the mechanics of grammar' (Lado 1957).

So Lado quite clearly recognizes the ability to communicate as the primary objective of language learning and conceives of structural practice only as a means to that end. The essential difference between his position and that of those who advocate communicative language teaching would seem to lie not in any disagreement about the centrality of communicative purpose but in the concept of communication itself. And this difference necessarily leads to different proposals as to how the ability to communicate should be taught.

Lado talks of 'the message conveyed through the language', and of 'the meaning of the communication' as linguistically encoded. It would appear from this that he conceives of meaning as intrinsic to language itself, a property signalled through the medium of language. This medium concept, which defines meaning as a function of the linguistic sign as formal symbol, can be contrasted with a concept of meaning as significance which is mediated by human agency. In this latter view, meaning is not a semantic matter of encoding and decoding messages by reference to linguistic knowledge but a pragmatic matter of negotiating an indexical relationship between linguistic signs and features of the context. It is not transmitted through the semantic *medium* of language, it is achieved by the pragmatic *mediation* of language users. So the question is not what linguistic expressions communicate but how do people communicate by using linguistic expressions. The medium account of meaning is therefore associated with the semantics of sentence grammar, the mediation account with the pragmatics of language use, as discussed in Part 2.

Pedagogic approaches: medium and mediation

What we have seen in language teaching, as in the study of language, over recent years is a shift of emphasis from the medium to the mediation view. An approach to pedagogy informed by the medium view will focus attention on the syntactic and semantic properties of the language itself and look for ways of manipulating them for the purposes of transmission. Learner activity will be directed at increasing receptivity. They will be involved in activities which are designed to facilitate the internalization of units of meaning so that they are put in store, so to speak, ready for use when required. Such activities will typically be *exercises* for the provision of practice. An approach informed by the mediation view will focus attention on creating conditions for negotiation. The learners will be engaged in activities designed to achieve purposeful outcomes by *means* of language. The activities here will be typically *tasks* for problem solving.

These two perspectives on meaning can, then, be quite naturally associated with different approaches to pedagogy, different ways of defining the language to be learned as a subject on the curriculum. Although these approaches may not determine practice in any absolute way, they can nevertheless be characterized in terms of certain interrelated tendencies.

Comparison of approaches

The medium perspective will tend to see the syllabus as primary since it is here that linguistic units are specified and ordered. These units may be given a formal or notional or functional definition but they are in all cases presented as packages of meaning. The assumption is that once they are taken into psychic store they are ready to be issued as ready-made tokens of communication. Methodology is essentially subservient, directed at facilitating this internalization process. In this respect, structural and notional/functional syllabuses are both informed by a medium view of communication, which is why it is so easy to rewrite one in terms of the other. With a mediation view, on the other hand, the methodology becomes primary. This is bound to be so since meaning can only be achieved by action and is not simply a reflex of knowledge. It is what learners actually do which results in meaning: communication is a function of activity which engages language for the achievement of purposeful outcomes. It is not surprising, therefore, that as the mediation view has taken hold, so the relevance of the syllabus has been redefined or called into question, even to the extent of denying the need for it altogether as a projected plan of work (see, for example, Candlin 1984).

The two perspectives will tend to see the organization of language for learning in very different terms. All pedagogy is involved in some kind of grading or ordering to allow for the gradual development of learning. The medium view will naturally provide for the gradual accumulation of units of meaning: it will be disposed to adopt the principle of text control, seeking to direct development by degrees. Since meaning is confined within language it has to be transmitted according to the channel capacity of the learner for the internalization of new linguistic forms. But in the mediation view meaning, of course, is not so confined. What this means is that if learners are prompted by a particular purpose, if they are oriented to some outcome or other, and are informed by relevant schematic knowledge, then they can be exposed to more language than they can process as sentences. The mediation view allows for ordering on the principle of task control, whereby language is regulated not by input but by intake. The channel capacity of the learners is increased by context. Meanings which are beyond the learners' linguistic competence to decipher by analysis are interpreted by inference, which is activated by communicative purpose and achieved by cross-reference to schematic knowledge. So the mediation perspective will favour a pedagogy of discovery whereby language is learned as a contingent consequence of carrying out activities which engage the language with the learners' knowledge and experience of other things. Whereas the text control of the medium view is a language filtering process, with the learner as recipient, the task control of the mediation view is a language focusing process, with the learner as agent.

Text control necessarily entails the contrivance of language teaching units, a pedagogic fabrication which shapes the raw materials of actually occurring language so as to make it simpler and more accessible. Task control, on the other hand, will tend to favour the presentation of language in its natural state and advocate the cause of authenticity.

These two perspectives on meaning will be inclined to conceive of the roles of teacher and learner in different terms. In the medium view, the learner is dependent on the teacher as a source of information. The teacher's task is to transmit, the learner's to receive what is transmitted. The process of transmission is seen as the same as the process of learning. Since meaning is encoded and decoded in the foreign language which the teacher knows and the learner does not, the learners' previous experience of meaning in the mother tongue is irrelevant. Indeed it is a nuisance since it is likely to act as a disruptive influence on learning. But if one takes a mediation view, the matter is altogether different. Learners already know how to use language to mediate meaning. They can draw on their own experience and employ the same sort of procedures to achieve meaning in the new language as those they use to achieve meaning in the mother tongue. The learner experience is not now an interference to be eliminated but a resource to be exploited. Accordingly, the learner assumes a more positive role. Learning is not now seen as conformity to the conditions of transmission controlled by the teacher but as a self-generating process by the learners themselves.

This difference of role relates closely to a fourth difference of principle between the two views. If meaning is thought of as signalled uniquely through the medium of language, then any departure from the rules of the language will result in a distortion of meaning, and communication will accordingly be impaired. So a medium view necessarily sets a high premium on correctness, and learner errors are seen as failures to internalize the devices necessary for the proper formulation of meaning. They are defective sentences. The mediation view, on the contrary, sees these nonconformist features of learner behaviour as positive signs of successful learning since they show the learner employing procedures for using whatever linguistic resources they have to hand to mediate meaning. These so-called errors may be defective sentences from the medium point of view, but effective utterances from the mediation point of view.

In summary, there are two ways of conceiving the nature of meaning, and these can be seen as informing different perspectives on language teaching, two pedagogic paradigms if you will.

One focuses on meaning as transmitted through the medium of language. It will concentrate on the devising of syllabuses of preplanned schemes of work based on text control whereby learners are directed by the teacher into the gradual reception of units of meaning. If the learners conform to these conditions of pedagogic transmission then they will learn the language as the code for the transmission of meaning. Nonconformity is negatively evaluated as error. The other perspective focuses on methodology, the instigation of classroom activity, allows for more exposure to language by guiding the learner by means of task control, provides for the exploitation of previous experience and for the exercise of initiative on the part of the learner. Nonconformity is positively evaluated as the achievement of an interim interlanguage.

Two paradigms, then, two sets of pedagogic principles identifiable by a consistency with a particular view of the nature of communication: either as the transmission of meaning by the semantic medium of language or as the achievement of meaning by the pragmatic mediation of the language user.

It is, of course, the mediation view which has become prominent over the past fifteen years. There are a number of reasons for this. For one thing, language teaching has been sensitive to developments in the study of language: the extension of the scope of linguistic description beyond the sentence, the study of actually occurring language in context, the interest in speech acts and pragmatics. At the same time, work in second language acquisition has suggested that it is the creative exploitation of language to achieve purposeful outcomes which generates the learning process itself. Both language use and language learning, it would appear, are to be characterized in terms of mediation.

There is another influence at work as well. The medium view is associated with authority. With its emphasis on transmission and conformity, it promotes the conservation of established social values and is consistent with a concept of education as the means of maintaining conventions and persuading people into their acceptance. Such an ideology is not well suited to the spirit of the age, at least as this is perceived in some parts of the world. It has been called into question on the grounds that it perpetuates the rule of privilege and denies the rights of self-determination and dissent. The mediation view is obviously more attuned to more liberal ideas, allowing as it does for discovery and self-expression. It emphasizes initiative rather than initiation, the autonomy of learning rather than the authority of teaching. Its consistency with what would seem to be a more enlightened social and educational ideology might seem reason enough to accept it as self-evidently preferable without further question. And some people, it would appear, have accepted it on these grounds, inspired by the humanistic fervour of the times.

Is there then nothing to be said for the medium perspective on pedagogy? Is it to be dismissed as entirely discredited? We may accept that communication is not semantic, a matter of deciphering, of encoding and decoding meaning in sentences; but we should note that this deciphering does demonstrate a knowledge of linguistic resources which are indispensable in the achievement of meaning by mediation. The language constitutes, in Halliday's terms, a meaning *potential*, and this can be manifested through sentences and so internalized. But the potential also needs to be *realized* as use, related to context, made actual, externalized as a purposeful outcome by mediation. It is not enough that the learner knows linguistic resources as an internalized potential, he must also know how to access this knowledge and realize it as a resource. Knowledge of language is a necessary condition for communication but it is not, as Lado seemed to imply, a sufficient condition. Language is a medium for the demonstration of meaning potential but this can only be *realized* by mediation.

It follows from this that the two perspectives (like the two approaches to language description outlined in Chapters 5–7, to which they relate) can be seen as being not in conflict but complementary so long as they do not make (as they sometimes seem to do) exclusive claims to truth. The meaning which is present as potential within linguistic forms serves as a set of bearings for the language user. It sets the guidelines, the parameters with reference to which meanings can be achieved by mediation. Language users cannot spin meanings out of nothing any more than they can achieve communicative purposes simply by reciting sentences.

Complementary approaches

Now what we have here I think is a very general principle of mutual dependency which we can apply to the other aspects of pedagogy I have referred to as associated with the two different perspectives on meaning. Consider, for example, the relationship between syllabus and methodology. One needs to allow methodological flexibility so that the opportunities for learning can be exploited as they emerge. But learn is a transitive verb: one has to learn *something* and this logically entails a measure of conformity to some scheme of things prefigured in advance. The most effective way of formulating a scheme of things, the object of learning, is to design a syllabus. This then serves as the necessary frame of reference. As far as language teaching is concerned, it seems to me that the syllabus is a device for specifying meaning potential as incorporated within linguistic units and it is the methodology which realizes this potential by mediating activities. It makes no more sense to attempt to account for mediation within a syllabus than it does to make methodology simply the means for manifesting the units of the language that the syllabus specifies. What one needs to do is to establish the proper concern of each aspect of the pedagogic process so that they can be effectively complementary. This matter is dealt with in some detail in Chapter 9.

Or consider the matter of allowing for the exercise of learner initiative. There is no doubt that the imposition of correctness, which is consistent with a medium view of meaning, has the effect of inhibiting the learners' engagement of relevant procedures for mediation acquired through an experience of their own language. There is no doubt that so-called errors are indeed evidence of the learners' success in realizing meaning potential. But they are also evidence of limitations in the learners' knowledge of meaning potential as encoded in the language they are learning. Learners therefore need to be provided with guidance in order to extend the range of the knowledge they can draw upon. This does not mean that they have to be subjected to direct correction, for this, being a shift from realization to manifestation, has the effect of undermining efforts at mediation, but it is perfectly possible to refer learners to correct forms and to set tasks which constrain their use without compromising the achievement of purposeful outcomes. Again, the question is how to create conditions for more effective mediation by referring the learners to the meaning potential they must exploit which is encoded within the language itself. One way in which this might be done is discussed in Chapter 10.

I have suggested that the pedagogic movement of the seventies and eighties that goes under the banner of communicative language teaching can be characterized not by a novel concern for communication but by a different conception of the nature of communication from that which prevailed in the preceding era. The tendency has been to suppose that since meaning is not uniquely signalled by language itself but is achieved by mediation, then all that is necessary is for learners to be involved in problem-solving tasks without explicit reference to the formal resources for meaning intrinsic in the language. My argument is that there needs to be *explicit* reference, that it is the purpose of pedagogy to actualize the mutual dependency between linguistically coded potential and its realization.

To do this is to recognize that the learners are not by the very nature of their role free agents: their agency is bound to be delimited. They cannot be charged with the sole responsibility for their own learning. It is to recognize, too, that there is no point in a pedagogy which does not intervene, does not exercise authority, does not set the limits which define the subject. Such a pedagogy, indeed, would be a contradiction in terms. The central issue is how to apply these constraints or limitations so that they constitute enabling conditions which facilitate the learning process rather than restrictions which inhibit it. What we need to consider, then, is how the roles of teacher and learner can be made effectively complementary so that effective learning comes about as a consequence of their interaction. This is an issue that is taken up in Chapter 11.

9 The problems and principles of syllabus design

Pedagogic and educational aspects of the syllabus

In order to avoid confusion (or at least to reduce it) I had better begin by making clear what I mean by the concept I intend to talk about in this chapter. I shall take a syllabus to mean the specification of a teaching programme or pedagogic agenda which defines a particular subject for a particular group of learners. Such a specification not only provides a characterization of content, the formalization in pedagogic terms of an area of knowledge or behaviour, but also arranges this content in a succession of interim objectives. A syllabus specification, then, is concerned with both the selection and the ordering of what is to be taught (cf. Halliday, McIntosh, and Strevens 1964; Mackey 1965). Conceived of in this way, a syllabus is an idealized schematic construct which serves as reference for teaching.

My main concern in this chapter is with the syllabus as the formulation of pedagogic goals. But it is important to recognize that the syllabus is also an instrument of educational policy. The goals are formulated not only in reference to pedagogic effectiveness but also in accordance with ideological positions concerning the nature of education in general, what Clark refers to as 'educational value systems' (1987).

Formal education can be defined as a superimposed second-order culture which consists of schemes of conceptual organization and behaviour designed to supplement the first-order processes of the primary socialization of family upbringing. As such its purpose is to give ideas, attitudes, actions, beliefs, and so on, a shape which they would not otherwise have, so as to prepare learners to participate in areas of social life beyond their immediate environment and to extend the range of their individual experience.

The relative weighting which is given to each of these general educational provisions, for future social role on the one hand and for personal development on the other, will depend on how different policies interpret the general purposes of education. Some, for example, will focus attention on future social role, define this in specific occupational terms, and seek to direct the curriculum towards the satisfaction of projected manpower needs. In this case, syllabuses will be designed to be accountable to measures of utility and will be, to use terms borrowed from Bernstein, 'position-oriented'. Syllabuses to meet the needs of English (or any other language) for specific purposes would be of this kind. Other policies will be more favourably disposed towards the individual, allow for a greater degree of divergence and self-realization and incline to 'person-orientation' (see Bernstein 1971).

The syllabus realizes educational policy and at the same time is realized by pedagogic methodology. What happens when the two are incompatible? Consider, for example, a case where educational policy is designed to prepare pupils to fit into an established social order. Such a position-oriented policy would set a high premium on conformity, and this would be incompatible with a methodology which was person-oriented and encouraged independent initiatives in learning. Conversely, one might have good reason to suppose that a person-oriented methodology with an emphasis on task-based discovery is to be favoured on the grounds that it is more effective in the promotion of learning. But this might run counter to a prevailing position-oriented educational policy which called for conformity and submission to teacher control.

As I argue later in this chapter, the teacher is not bound to interpret the syllabus in line with its intentions: methodology can always find some room for manoeuvre. Nevertheless the influence of policy is powerful and cannot be disregarded, particularly, of course, because examinations assess the syllabus which embodies it, and not the methodology. Furthermore, to the extent that policy is informed by an established educational orthodoxy, it is likely to reflect prevailing expectations and attitudes on the part of both teachers and learners, not only in respect of the language subject but also in respect of other subjects on the curriculum. One cannot expect that learners will take readily to modes of behaviour in the language class which are at variance with those which are promoted in their other lessons.

The general point to be made relates to the discussion in the second chapter of this book: it is that pedagogic proposals have always to be referred to socio-cultural factors in particular educational settings. Whatever good reasons there may be for adopting a pedagogy of person-orientation, one has to recognize that there are societies, and educational systems which serve them, for which this is a dangerous doctrine. The design of a syllabus and its implementation by means of methodology can never be simply a pedagogic matter. Having noted this point, we can now go on to consider this matter of implementation.

Syllabus and methodology

The task for teacher is to realize the syllabus as a course of action by whatever methodological means seem most appropriate for the activation of learning. The syllabus itself is an inert abstract object. It has much the same relationship to learner activities as does any abstract model of knowledge to the actuality of behaviour. Its function is not to provide a prospectus of everything that the learner has to do. It is, so to speak, a set of bearings for teacher action and not a set of instructions for learner activity. What learners do is not directly determined by the syllabus but is a consequence of how the syllabus is methodologically mediated by the teacher in the pursuit of his own course of instruction.

It follows from this that changes in syllabus as such need have no effect on learning whatever. They will only do so if they inspire the teacher to introduce methodological innovations in the planning and execution of activities in the classroom which are consistent in some way with the conception of content and the principle of ordering proposed in the new syllabus. The main purpose of syllabus reform, in this view, is therefore to alter the perspectives of teachers, shift their customary points of reference and so provide them with a different set of guidelines. Unless teachers clearly understand what principles inform these guidelines and how they can be acted upon by means of an appropriate methodology which promotes learning activities, then new syllabus proposals are likely to remain in the region of wishful thinking and pious hope, interesting ideas for academic debate but ineffectual in the domain of pedagogic practice. The effect of a syllabus on pedagogic practice depends on the effective appraisal and application of the ideas that inform it (see Chapter 3).

Failure to recognize that the syllabus as a source of teacher reference can only effect learning through methodological mediation has led, I think, to the mistaken (but quite common) assumption that a notional/functional syllabus is synonymous with a communicative approach to language teaching and that, more generally, communicative pedagogy is primarily a matter of syllabus design. But a notional/functional syllabus is of itself no more communicative than is a 'structural' one. Communication is what may or not be achieved through classroom activity; it cannot be embodied in an abstract specification. Of course, as I have already said, teachers may be inspired to realize the implications of a particular way of specifying content and its arrangement. But equally, they can ignore such implications, or not recognize them, and proceed to teach in reference to a notional/ functional syllabus in just the same way as they previously taught in reference to a structural one.

Conversely, it is perfectly possible to adopt a communicative methodology in the realization of a syllabus designed along structural lines. So I do not see that there is anything paradoxical or perverse in saying that there is no such thing as a communicative syllabus (see Stern 1984). The assumption that there is, or can be, has, it seems to me, tended to deflect attention from the real issues of communicative pedagogy which are essentially methodological in character, and which therefore relate crucially to the mediating role of the teacher.

Ways of characterizing and ordering the content units of a language syllabus do not, then, determine classroom activity (for a discussion see Johnson 1979; Breen 1987). But they may carry implications about what activities might effectively be promoted as consistent with the syllabus rationale. It is of interest to enquire, therefore, what principles appear to inform different approaches to syllabus design, and what implications might be drawn from them for methodological practice.

The specification of syllabus content

In the approach to the definition of the language subject which was orthodox until recent times, the characterization of content was derived from formal models of linguistic description: the units for teaching were assumed to be the same as the units of grammar. Latterly, in accordance with a different orthodoxy, characterization has been in reference to the concepts and actions (notions and functions) which these formal elements most commonly realize when language knowledge is put to use. What motivates this change of perspective? Mainly, it would seem, considerations not of language *learning* but of language *use*. The reason for defining language content in terms of notional/functional rather than formal structural units is that these are seen as being more immediately relevant to what learners will need eventually to *do* with the language once they have learned it. The emphasis is on the objectives and not the procedures of language learning, on purpose not process. It is a needs or goal-oriented rationale, expressed by Wilkins in the following way:

> The process of deciding what to teach is based on consideration of what the learner should most usefully be able to communicate in the foreign language.   *(1976: 19)*

It would seem to follow that such a characterization is also based on the assumption that learning behaviour must be some sort of *pre-scripted rehearsal* for actual use. The implication for teaching is that methodology should ensure that classroom language is as close an approximation to authentic language behaviour as possible. In this way, the learner accumulates a performance repertoire for subsequent enactment when required.

This goal-oriented rehearsal assumption runs directly counter to that which informs the characterization of syllabus content in structural terms. It is not that the structural syllabus denies the eventual communicative purpose of learning but that it implies a different means to its achievement. It is often suggested that the designers of such syllabuses supposed that language was of its nature entirely reducible to elements of formal grammar and failed to recognize the reality of use. But this, as I have pointed out in Chapter 8, is a misrepresentation. Such syllabuses were proposed as a means towards achieving language performance through the skills of speaking, listening, reading, and writing. That is to say, they were directed towards a communicative goal and were intended, no less than the notional/functional syllabus, as a preparation for use. The difference lies in the conception of the means to this end. 'Structural' syllabuses are designed on the assumption that it is the internalization of grammar coupled with the exercise of linguistic skills in motor-perceptive manipulations (usage) which affords the most effective preparation for the reality of communicative encounters (use). The content of such syllabuses, therefore, is not conceived of as units of performance, bits of pre-scripted communicative behaviour, to be accumulated and issued like tokens when future occasions arise. The content comprises units of linguistic competence, made manifest as usage in spoken and written sentences but making no claim to the status of natural utterance. Their learning constitutes an investment in competence (and not an accumulation of performance capital) to be variously realized to meet unpredictable requirements in the future.

In general terms the underlying implications behind the two approaches to syllabus design might be formulated as follows. The notional/functional syllabus implies that the subject language is to be taught as units of communicative performance for accumulation. The structural syllabus implies that the subject is to be taught as units of linguistic competence for investment.

It is interesting to note, in this connection, that in the first volume of *English Language Teaching* published in 1946, the editor A.S. Hornby provides examples of language teaching techniques and makes it quite clear that these are not designed to have any communicative validity: 'None of the material given above can be described as "conversation". It is oral drill, and even the expanded answers in the later stages are mechanical. Real conversation cannot be taught in the artificial atmosphere of the classroom and we may as well recognize the fact.'

But Hornby would of course have claimed that this mechanistic process contributes to the eventual purpose of achieving the ability to communicate. His position is the same as that of Lado, referred to in Chapter 8. Teaching language *for* communication as an end is not the same as teaching language *as* communication as a means (see Widdowson 1984a: Paper 16).

Now it will be evident that although these two perspectives on the language subject are commonly represented as in opposition, they are really complementary, each compensating for the limitations of the other. We need the communicative orientation of one combined with the competence orientation of the other. Communicative ability must clearly incorporate competence of some kind and cannot just be a performance repertoire. The syllabus has to allow for the investment of knowledge for future and unpredictable realization. With regard to the notional/functional syllabus, therefore, we need to dissociate communication from accumulation. The structural syllabus provides us with the investment principle we want, but this is associated with the formal properties of the language and, as is evident from past experience, this sort of investment is not readily realized as communicative behaviour. With regard to the structural syllabus, therefore, we need to dissociate investment from linguistic forms as such, and apply it to communicative function. We might summarize these general points in the following way:

syllabus type	content unit	learning principle	learning consequence
structural	formal	investment	linguistic competence
N/F	functional	accumulation	communicative performance

Figure 2

An interesting question arises here with respect to these principles of investment and accumulation, namely the extent to which an adherence to the former principle necessarily entails an analytic concept of content, and an adherence to the latter principle a holistic one. Certainly the units of a structural syllabus are discrete items of analysed knowledge, as Bialystok defines it, and she seems to associate this with investment with regard to language proficiency:

> The assumption is that if knowledge is analysed, then certain *uses* may be made of that knowledge which cannot be made of knowledge which is unanalysed. (1982: 183)

Of course, as I noted in Chapter 6, a good deal of the native speaker's knowledge of language remains unanalysed as holistic conglomerate units or formulas which resist analysis by rule application (see Bolinger 1976; Pawley and Syder 1983) and there is a good deal of compelling evidence that first and second language learners invest in such formulas in the process of learning (see Peters 1983; Vihman 1982). We should be careful, therefore, to allow for the acquisition of unanalysed knowledge as an aspect of competence and not assume, as the structural approach tended to do, that investment necessarily entails analysis.

Interestingly, Wilkins associates analysis with the notional/functional syllabus and refers to the structural syllabus as synthetic (Wilkins 1976). But he uses these terms, it would seem, not to characterize the nature of the content itself but what teachers and learners do with it. Thus, according to Wilkins, the teacher who works from a structural syllabus is constrained to an incremental presentation of the discretely ordered items so as to synthesize them in the learner's mind as knowledge, whereas working from a notional/functional syllabus will require the presentation of language as holistic chunks of behaviour, leaving the learner to do the necessary analysis.

So a synthetic syllabus is one which presents language as analysed units to be synthesized in the process of learning whereas an analytic syllabus presents language as synthesized units to be analysed in the process of learning. We have, then, in principle, a clear distinction: two competing approaches to pedagogy, informed by diametrically opposed theories of learning. What is not clear, however, is how this distinction is exemplified by the structural syllabus on the one hand and the notional/functional syllabus on the other, as Wilkins describes them.

It is not obvious, for example, why the sentences which serve as the basic units of a structural syllabus are any more analytic in character than the speech acts or communicative expressions which are the basic units of the notional/functional syllabus. The two kinds of unit would appear to be exactly isomorphic, the one being a functional variant of the other. Consider an example:

Shall we go to the zoo?

This, says Wilkins, is an example of the category of communicative function of suasion; more specifically its use is to carry out the act of suggestion. Exactly the same combination of words might appear in a structural syllabus. But here it would be presented not as an act of suggestion but as one type of interrogative sentence. But in both cases we have a collection of words synthesized into a larger unit. They differ only in the way the unit is conceived: formally on the one hand, functionally on the other. And in both cases there is need for analysis if the expression is to be taken as an example of how the language works rather than as a fixed phrase without any generative potential. That is to say, formally the learners will need to devise other interrogative sentences with different lexical items and syntactic constituents, and functionally to make other suggestions for carrying out different activities.

Of course, the *kind* of analysis will be very different. With regard to the interrogative form, it is a matter of identifying the device of subject/auxiliary verb reversal in English, of inferring the contrast:

Shall we go to the zoo?
We shall go to the zoo.

This might then lead on to further analysis of the verb, the recognition of the need to isolate tense from its lexical connections and provide it with its own form in interrogative sentences of this sort. Thus, we might infer the following contrasts:

We went to the zoo.
*Went we to the zoo?
Did we go to the zoo?

With regard to the expression of suggestion, analysis would be a matter of identifying this modal auxiliary in association with the first person plural pronoun as the realization of this particular function, so that the following, for example, do not have the same functional potential:

Will we go to the zoo?
Shall I go to the zoo?

So whether this combination of words is being presented as a formal or a functional unit of meaning, the learner needs to analyse out the first two words as a separate component which has transferable signifying potential. The difference lies not in the *degree* but in the *kind* of analysis which is applied.

It is possible to conceive of syllabuses which are designed in accordance with the opposing principles that Wilkins suggests, but which would be different from the structural and notional/functional types that he describes. In reference to the broad distinction which was made in Part 2 between semantic and pragmatic approaches to language description, we might propose, for example, that a synthetic syllabus is one which works semantically from the inside out, so to speak, whereas the analytic syllabus is one which adopts the reverse, pragmatic procedure and works from the outside in.

Thus a synthetic syllabus would define its units in lexical terms and, along the lines suggested in Chapter 6, would gradually introduce elements of grammar as needed to modify words in association to make them more contextually effective. The synthesizing of words into syntactic structures would be motivated by communicative requirement. In this respect it would not just deal in formal manipulations of the kind usually associated with the structural syllabus, but in the realizations of meaning which are usually claimed to characterize the notional/ functional syllabuses. But it would be thoroughly synthetic in the Wilkins sense.

An analytic syllabus, on the other hand, would not be bottom-up but top-down. That is to say, it would present language in the form of larger textual units and set tasks of different kinds which would direct the learners' attention to specific features, formal or functional, of the language they were exposed to. Analysis would then be induced by means of controlled procedural work.

It is possible too to conceive of syllabuses which reconcile the opposing principles of synthesis and analysis. Crombie, for example, has put forward proposals for what she calls a relational approach to syllabus design (Crombie 1985). The basic unit here is the propositional relation (see also Widdowson 1979: Paper 20). This can operate within a sentence where it connects different constituents together, or it can operate across sentence-like elements of larger textual units. The propositional relation, therefore, operates both in the narrow domain favoured by the synthetic syllabus and the broader domain favoured by the analytic syllabus. For example:

The cancellation of the match was on account of the rain.

This propositional content can be unpacked, so to speak, and expressed in terms of a main and subordinate clause:

The match was cancelled because it was raining.

But the same cause and effect relationship between these events can be expressed by a variety of ways across separate elements of texts which are more or less contiguous, more or less explicitly connected. For example:

The match was cancelled. . . . . . . It was raining.
The match was cancelled. . . . . . . This was because of the rain.
It was raining. . . . . The match was cancelled.
It was raining. . . . . Because of this, the match was cancelled.

Where there is an absence of explicit signalling and the presence of intervening, potentially distracting, text (indicated by the dotted lines) there will be an increased dependence on the kind of interpretative procedures discussed in Chapter 7.

A syllabus based on the different realization of propositional relations could either proceed synthetically by projecting outwards from sentence to text, or analytically by focusing inwards from text to sentence.

What all this would seem to show is, as I indicated earlier, that syllabus type does not determine its mode of implementation in any particular methodology. I do not think it follows that learners who are practised in the use of formulaic units will necessarily analyse them so as to have their constituent parts accessible for other combinations and applicable in a general range of contexts. But now that methodological issues have come into the discussion, we need to consider them more closely.

Methodological implications of content specification

What kind of methodological practices would be consistent with the ideas about language and learning which are implied by these different approaches to syllabus design? A teacher using a notional/functional syllabus as reference, if she is sensitive to what is implied, will tend to promote activities in the classroom which have as much communicative verisimilitude as possible, so that they function effectively as rehearsal. She will favour materials which are 'authentic' as instances of use. Her methodology, in brief, will be behaviour-oriented. A teacher acting on the implications of a structural syllabus, on the other hand, will tend to promote activities which serve to internalize the formal properties of language and will accept the need for contrivance. Her methodology will be knowledge-oriented. The danger of the former methodology is that learners may accumulate performance units without being able to refer them to any underlying competence which alone can provide the sort of adaptable resource required for actual communication and for further learning. The danger of the latter methodology is that the learners may find that having made their speculative investment in form, they cannot gain effective access to it: they cannot act on their knowledge.

It seems clear that what is wanted is a methodology which will (in reference to the diagram on page 133) provide for communicative competence by functional investment. I have indicated elsewhere what such a methodology might involve (e.g. Widdowson 1983, 1984a and Chapter 10 in the present book). Very generally, it would engage the learners in problem-solving tasks as purposeful activities but without the rehearsal requirement that they should be realistic or 'authentic' as natural social behaviour. The process of solving such problems would involve a conscious and repeated reference to the formal properties of the language, not in the abstract, dissociated from use, but as a necessary resource for the achievement of communicative outcomes. Such a methodology makes a virtue out of the necessity of classroom contrivance and sees it not as a debilitating constraint but as a facilitating condition for the development of communicative competence in the language.

I will return to the matter of a problem-solving methodology later in relation to issues arising from the ordering of syllabus content. But for the present we need to note that such a methodology is not determined by a commitment to either of the syllabus types that have been discussed but depends on realizing a complementary relationship between them. It can either develop as a communicative complement to the principle of investment or as an investment complement to the idea of functional content. It does not matter which syllabus serves as the point of reference so long as the teacher can realize it appropriately in this complementary fashion in actual classroom activities. This is why so much discussion about the design of 'communciative' syllabuses is misdirected. Which kind of syllabus a teacher has to work with is relatively unimportant. This is fortunate since she very often has no choice in the matter anyway. What is important is that teachers should understand the principles underlying the characterization of content in a particular syllabus so that they might adopt or adapt these effectively in the area where they do have room for independent action, namely in the mediating activities of classroom methodology.

The ordering of syllabus content

Discussion so far has centred on the different ways that course content is characterized as defining what aspects of language might have pedagogic primacy in getting learners to acquire relevant proficiency as an eventual objective. We have yet to consider the question of how such content might be ordered so as to serve effectively the *process* of learning. I referred to ordering earlier as the specification of interim objectives. These can be conceived of in two ways. One is in terms of their surrender value or communicative pay-off in respect of practical use. This would yield a series of stages each representing a level in proficiency for use. The criteria for such staging relate to what is to be learned by what point in the way of realizable profit, as it were, and are determined by considerations of investment and so on which we have already dealt with in the discussion of the characterization of content. The second way of conceiving of ordering, however, has to do with language development as a function of the learning process itself. This is a very different matter.

The distinction I am making here between the different criteria for ordering corresponds, in my mind, with that familiar in testing between achievement and proficiency. Tests of achievement measure progress in learning. Since this progress is not an accumulation of standard forms but the development of a non-standard interlanguage, there is, or should be, no requirement in achievement tests that performance should match up to the norms of correctness or appropriateness associated with native speaker behaviour. Tests of proficiency, on the other hand, measure the ability to access and to act upon what has been learnt to realize effective communicative behaviour. Here learner performance clearly does have to be set against the norms of native speakers.

A central question in regard to ordering as a way of facilitating achievement (as distinct from ordering as a way of providing for levels of proficiency) is the extent to which content can be ordered so as to conform to, or at least be congruent with, the sequences which mark the natural process of learning. In a paper first published in 1979 (though reprinted since), Corder made the following remarks:

Efficient language teaching must work with, rather than against, natural processes, facilitate and expedite rather than impede learning. Teachers and teaching materials must adapt to the learner rather than vice versa. The study of interlanguage is the study of the natural processes of language learning. What has been discovered so far suggests that the nearer we can approximate language teaching to the learning of a second language in an informal setting the more successful we shall be.

And he goes on to derive from this the following practical proposal:

...the accommodation of the structure of our linguistic syllabuses and teaching materials to fit what is known of the sequence of progressive complication of the approximate systems of the free learner. (*1981: 77*)

If we accept that such accommodation is desirable (and this, as I have suggested in Chapter 3, is not as self-evident as it might seem to be) then the question arises as to whether (nearly ten years on) we now know enough about second language acquisition and natural emergence of interlanguage to be able to sequence content accordingly, thereby adapting the teacher's syllabus to conform to the 'built-in' syllabus of the learner, as Corder would wish.

The last ten years have seen a great proliferation of research into second language acquisition (SLA). The collection of papers published to honour Corder himself (Davies, Criper, and Howatt 1984) gives a good indication of its scope and subtlety, as does the synthesis provided by Ellis (1985). This research has yielded an abundance of fascinating facts and speculations about the language learning process and its possible determinants. What it has not yielded is anything so specific as a definitive linear succession of items that defines interlanguage development, and which could directly inform content order in a syllabus.

Indeed there would appear to be good evidence in support of the intuitive conviction that natural learning does not proceed strictly in this linear fashion anyway (see Long 1985: 79 and the references cited there). The indications are of an emergence of certain salient features of language, resembling general principles, rather than the precise formation of rules, which follow a development sequence of an implicational kind with one feature following dependently on the previous appearance of another. But at no regular intervals. This is because in between these appearances, other features may intervene in no fixed order playing out a supporting role. To account for this variable emergence, Ellis has proposed a distinction between *order* and *sequence* of acquisition. The former is the succession without fixed intervals of the more general organizing principles or salient features of grammar, and the latter is the succession of these together with other features appearing without predetermined order in linear arrangement (Ellis 1985: 64). This proposal incidently has interesting parallels with the structural analysis of folktales and myths where the objective is to identify the underlying (and perhaps universal) order of elements through the varying sequences of particular events which appear in different narratives.

We should note, therefore (to return to the relatively non-fictional world of second language acquisition research), that if any stable and generalizable findings do eventually emerge from such research, they can, if this current hypothesis is sustained, only relate to order (in Ellis's terms) and not to sequence. So they could not provide criteria for any precise specification but only for a more general staging of content, motivated though by learning needs and a concern for achievement rather than by the requirement for a usable communicative return and a concern for proficiency. Syllabus design based on such findings would presumably consist of a series of general parameters representing the established implicational sequence of general grammatical principles, subsequently given more specific realization by methodological means, involving the incidental inclusion of other features.

Two further points might be made in reference to this question as to whether content arrangement in a syllabus might be informed by findings relating to the natural growth of language in the learner's mind. The first has to do with the observation made earlier that there is no necessary correspondence between achievement in learning and proficiency in use. Achievement progresses through the approximative systems of interlanguage and, as Pienemann points out, to model a syllabus on this progression would involve the inclusion of interlanguage forms which, by definition, do not conform to the rules of the standard language (see Pienemann 1985). The assumption that a syllabus should only include correct instances of language runs counter to the notion that it should be fashioned to correspond with the in-built syllabus of the natural learner. Bearing in mind that syllabuses are designed as *teaching* specifications and generally prescribed by educational authorities, it is highly unlikely, even if it were deemed to be pedagogically desirable, that a syllabus which specified deviant forms as teaching items would find much institutional favour.

A second point has to do with how linguistic knowledge is to be defined. Studies in second language acquisition have generally defined it in terms of the internalization of morpho-syntactic rules of the language system (see Ellis 1985: 288–9). What is not clear, though, is how freely available such rules are in respect to different lexical realization and contextual function. A learner may know certain rules but only within a limited range of application. She may know them as they are associated with a certain set of lexical items but not be able to generalize them to others; she may know them as they are used to realize certain communicative functions but not be able to extend them into other domains of use. In short, the rules may only be known in relative degrees of analysability and accessibility (see again Bialystok 1982).

Considerations such as these lend support to Selinker's belief in the need to bring together the fields of second language acquisition and language for special purposes (LSP) (see, for example, Selinker 1984; Selinker and Douglas 1985). In LSP we are concerned (among other things) with how the discourse conventions which characterize different domains of use are textualized by particular choices of the lexis and grammar of the language in question. Thus it might be demonstrated that a certain rhetorical function in one discourse domain is typically realized by means of a particular tense (see Trimble 1985). It would be the purpose of an LSP course to establish the relationship between tense and function in this domain. But there is no guarantee that the learner would be able to dissociate this tense from the lexical and contextual connections which define this function so that it was freely transferable to other functions and other domains. It could be learned only as the element of a relatively restricted formula. In other domains, the learner might make use of other forms in his interlanguage repertoire. This particular tense would, then, be only partially acquired as a contextual variant. But an LSP syllabus which was designed to provide only for the use of language in this particular domain would not of its nature make provision for any extension of this restricted range.

It is worth pointing out, however, that variable competence is not only to be associated with the interlanguage of learners. It is a fact of life for native speakers also. They too may be able to access certain areas of knowledge in recognition for receptive purposes but fail to access them in recall for production. They may know certain words as they appear in certain phrases and as they relate to certain contexts but be unable to use them in free transference. All language knowledge is only relatively analysed and accessible: a good deal of it, as I indicated earlier, takes the form of conglomerate units and is contextually tagged.

All languages reveal the co-existence of lexical and syntactic variants which are associated with different functions, forms which are semantically equivalent but pragmatically distinguishable, appropriate in some contexts but not in others. So when the language learners develop context related variants in their interlanguage, they are following their natural instincts as language users in a way we would wish to encourage as evidence of communicative competence. The only problem is that the learners' variants are deviations from the standard norm, and in this respect are evidence of linguistic incompetence.

It is clear from all this that if SLA research is to yield anything of relevance to syllabus design which is directed at the development of communicative competence, then it will need to define its object of enquiry so as to take into account the natural language phenomenon of contextual variability (see Ellis 1985: Chapter 4; Tarone 1988).

What we need to know, then, is how learners extend the range of application of the rules they internalize, how they develop in making use of 'procedures for accessing the knowledge' (Bialystok and Sharwood-Smith 1985). This would clearly have a bearing on the arrangement of syllabus content. Instead of arranging items in some absolute sequence, assuming that once the item was learned in one lexical and contextual environment, it would transfer automatically to all others, we could instead order content cyclically in terms of an increasing range of application, requiring of methodology that it should provide activities which develop the necessary accessing procedures.

Methodological implications of content ordering

Work on second language acquisition gives us (as yet at least) little in the way of reliable guidance as far as syllabus design is concerned. So what pedagogic relevance does it have? The question brings us back once more to the primacy of methodological considerations. The factors which bear upon natural language acquisition are clearly many and complex, but they can be grouped under two main headings. There are those which constitute *essential conditions*. These are of a cognitive character and they set the psychic co-ordinates, as it were, of natural language development. The second sort of factors are of a communicative character and these trigger off or activate the developmental process, and provide the *enabling conditions* for growth by providing an experience of language. Now if we cannot fashion a syllabus to incorporate the essential conditions of the natural learning process what we can do is create these enabling conditions in the classroom by means of a methodology which allows the learner to acquire language as a function of natural language behaviour.

It is this kind of thinking that informs the 'natural approach' (Krashen and Terrell 1983) and, in a different and more rigorous way, the work of Prabhu in South India (Prabhu 1985, 1987; Johnson 1982; Brumfit 1984a). For Krashen, as we have seen (see Chapter 2), natural language behaviour seems to involve little more than the reception of comprehensible input, which he confidently proclaims to be, '*the* [sic] fundamental pedagogical principle in second language teaching' (Krashen 1981). This principle, the Input Hypothesis, is formulated as follows:

1   We acquire by understanding input language that contains structures a bit beyond our current level of competence.
2   Speech is a result of acquisition, not a cause.
3   If input is understood, and there is enough of it, the necessary grammar is automatically provided. (*1983: 159*)

Prabhu also believes that grammar is acquired as a function of meaning realization, but accepts the need for more active involvement on the part of the learner whereby meaning is achieved in the process of problem solving. For Krashen, it would appear, the input acts upon the mind, and this serves as a sufficient catalyst. How the act of comprehension is actually achieved is not considered. Nor, for that matter is the issue of analysability and the possibility of a restricted range of application as discussed earlier. For Prabhu, on the other hand, it is the intellectual effort of reasoning which sets the internal cognitive process of acquisition into motion. The mind acts upon the input. Although in both cases the assumption is that involvement with meaningful uses of language will be effective in developing grammatical competence, Prabhu's approach provides for analysis as a condition of conscious learning.

The kind of task which Prabhu found to be most effective was one which involved what he calls 'reasoning-gap activities'. Such an activity 'involves deriving some new information from given information through processes of inference, deduction, practical reasoning, or a perception of relationships or patterns' (1987: 47). Such an activity is more likely of its very nature to lead to an analytic abstraction of intrinsic meanings in language than is the passive exposure to input that Krashen would seem to advocate, which relies on the activation of the language acquisition device without the learners' rational involvement. Another reason for Prabhu's preference for reasoning-gap activities is that it allows for teacher intervention and the control of learning:

> When a reasoning-gap activity proves difficult for learners, the teacher is able to guide their efforts step by step, making the reasoning explicit or breaking it down into smaller steps, or offering parallel instances to particular steps.   *(1987: 48)*

Interestingly enough, this bears a marked resemblance to the methodology of what Prabhu calls the structural-oral-situational (S.O.S.) approach and which his procedural pedagogy is quite explicitly intended to replace. The difference is, of course, that in Prabhu's proposals the methodology is not applied to the language itself but to problem-solving activities which are designed to induce language contingently. Even so, such explicit focusing on the elements of the problem is, one would think, bound to direct attention to the elements of language in which they are expressed. One might draw a parallel with the kind of problems which are set in the teaching of mathematics (and indeed the task which Prabhu describes involving the use of railway timetables could be readily adapted to such a purpose). In this case learners would need to apply mathematical rather than linguistic procedures as a means to the solution. But they would at the same time be learning the use of algebraic equations and other formal devices for calculation. It seems reasonable to suggest that the use of the formal devices of language would be learned in a comparable way.

At all events, it is clear that the methodology of the Prabhu approach is not one which simply allows natural acquisition to take its course by undirected discovery or the instinctive reaction to input. Monitoring is much in evidence. It is for this reason that he describes it as learn*ing*- but not learn*er*-centered (see Prabhu 1985).

Although there are differences between them, the approaches adopted by Krashen and Prabhu are both based on an assumption which runs directly counter to that which informs the design of a structural syllabus. Rather than supposing that a grammatical investment (demonstration and practice) will yield a communicative return, the assumption here is that a communicative investment (input or interaction) will yield a grammatical return. In reference to the distinction made earlier the rationale for communicative methodology relates here not to the goal but to the process of learning: it is based not on the accumulation but on the investment principle.

The view here is that the activation of natural acquisition will be sufficient, without the deliberate teacher inducement of conscious learning by directing the attention of learners to form. It is a view that not everybody feels disposed to share. Brumfit, for one, does not.

> A consequence of the view that learning does not assist acquisition is the dismissal of several traditional learning activities as peripheral. Examples are exercises and drills and grammatical explanation procedures . . . and an authoritative rejection of such procedures needs to be based on firmer evidence than has been forthcoming.   *(1984a: 320)*

The role of the syllabus

These are not the only pedagogic traditions which are called into question by the transfer of power, so to speak, from teacher to learner, by the reliance placed on natural acquisition rather than directed learning. The teacher's authority for direction, the syllabus itself, becomes vulnerable. Since it cannot be fashioned to model the acquisition process, it can only be an instrument of teacher imposition (no matter how benevolent) and so, it might be argued, it can and indeed should be dispensed with, at least as it is traditionally conceived. Instead one might retain the term but redefine it to mean not the projection of a scheme of work but a retrospective record of classroom activity, a product of the methodological process rather than a preconceived framework within which such a process can operate (see Candlin 1984).

One way of allowing for the initiative of the learner to plot his own course by following his natural flair is effectively to abandon altogether the traditional notion of syllabus. Another less extreme strategy is to redefine content not in terms of the forms or functions of language as such but in terms of problems of a conceptual or communicative character which require the use of language for their solution. This is the strategy favoured by Prabhu in his proposals for a so-called procedural syllabus. This can be seen (if this does not seem immodest) as a modification of the proposal I first put forward nearly twenty years ago (Widdowson 1968) and which is currently finding some belated favour, that language learning is most effectively promoted by the contingent use of the language in the study of other subjects on the curriculum.

It is important to note that this proposal is based on a process-oriented investment rationale rather than a goal-oriented accumulation one. This has not always been appreciated. Cook, for example, comments that 'Many language teachers would deny that their main purpose in teaching English was to enable their students to understand physics or geography in English.' (1983: 231)

But the point is that the subject is meant to create conditions for purposeful activity whereby the process of language learning is engaged: it does not constitute the unique goal of learning. The argument is that if learners have learned the language purposefully, then they will have invested in an ability which can be put to purposes beyond those which originally served to develop it. This in turn invests language teaching with an educational rather than a training purpose (see Widdowson 1983).

The modification of this subject-based proposal, as put forward by Prabhu, retains the investment principle but dissociates it from established curriculum subjects. What it essentially involves, therefore, is the devising of a subject (logical reasoning, for example) which applies activities associated with other subjects to neutral topics. This kind of problem solving, as a methodological procedure, was mentioned earlier in this chapter as a way of reconciling the apparently competing implications of structural and notional/functional syllabuses.

But the use of problem-solving tasks as units of syllabus content, as distinct from activities for syllabus realization, encounters a number of difficulties. By what criteria, for example, are such tasks to be sequentially arranged? If the sequence is to be in accord with natural learning, as it would be only consistent to require, then reliable information is needed about cognitive development at different stages of maturation, about the conditions, psychological and social, which attend the emergence in the mind of general problem-solving capabilities. Armed with such information, we could perhaps relate these capabilities to certain task types, analysed into their constituent features and then given token realizations and ranged in an order of increasing complexity. Such information is not, to my knowledge, currently available.

Suggestive findings relating to this issue have, however, emerged from general psychological research on child development. It seems clear, for example, that tasks increase in difficulty the more remote they are from the schematic knowledge of the children. Margaret Donaldson (1978) takes issue with Piaget on the question of the child's reasoning ability at about the age of five or six. Piaget's claim is that children at this age are incapable of reasoning out the relationship between classes and sub-classes of objects and offers the following evidence in support of his claim. When children are presented with two obvious sub-classes of a more general class, say four red flowers and two white flowers, they will fail to answer correctly a question of the kind:

Are there more red flowers or more flowers?

Children will regularly reply that there are more red flowers, But the reason for this may be that children are interpreting what they suppose to be a likely utterance rather than the actual words which are said. The question is an odd one which is unlikely to occur in the context of ordinary discourse. A more normal question would be:

Are there more red flowers or more white flowers?

In other words the children may be reforming the language to a model of their familiar world and this schematic knowledge overrides the specific sense of the words—a common phenomenon in language use, as we have seen from the discussion earlier in Chapter 7.

Donaldson points out that experiments show that when tasks are related more closely to the child's experience, when the reasoning is associated with familiar schemata and embedded in other and more purposeful activities, then the child reveals no such deductive deficiency.

We return here to issues concerning the negotiation of meaning raised in Part 2. There it was pointed out that the less schematic knowledge can be engaged in interpretation (itself a kind of problem solving of course), the more reliance will need to be placed on systemic knowledge, or knowledge of the language. Now it would seem that there is good reason to suppose that schooling in general through all subjects seeks to develop in children the capability for dealing with meanings in language which are not schema-derived, that is to say which are not dependent on the immediate context of experience. In reference to research carried out in Canada, for example, David Olson observes:

All of these studies suggest that schooling is responsible for an important reorientation to language, the differentiation of what the sentence means, its direct or 'sentence meaning'. It is my conjecture that schooled competence, including competence in intelligence tests, is based on the ability to respond to sentence meaning, the meaning in the syntactic and lexical structures of the sentence, or as I prefer to state it, to treat language as if the meaning were 'in the text'. The focus on language, on mastering and explicating the meanings in the language, takes many forms: formulating definitions of words, devising verbal rules, and drawing valid inferences. These are of course among the very intellectual effects associated with schooling. *(1981: 385)*

If Olson is right (and he acknowledges that what he says is conjecture) then the development of the problem-solving ability or conceptual competence in schoolchildren may not be distinct from the development of competence in the language. This would suggest in turn that task grading might be done in reference to degrees of schematic familiarity and dependence on meanings intrinsic to text. It would also suggest in reference to the points made earlier about Prabhu's methodology that a focusing on the elements of the reasoning-gap task might well, in practice, involve directing attention to the elements of language itself as a corollary.

At all events, we have (at the moment) no definite guidance on how tasks might be sequenced in terms of conceptual complexity or implicational dependence. So the proposal for a task-based syllabus, if it is to be concerned with the principled arrangement as well as the specification of content, runs into precisely the same problems as beset the proposal to model a syllabus on the sequence of natural language acquisition. Against this, it might be suggested that there is no need for such precision in task gradation, that a rough and intuitive calculation of complexity will do. But then how does one guard against intuition referring to linguistic criteria for such a calculation? And if the task ordering does not correspond with a natural order, then it can be argued that it will inhibit natural cognitive initiative in just the same way as an uninformed linguistic ordering constrains natural language development. Either way, the result is just the sort of imposition and interference in learning processes which it is the very purpose of a procedural syllabus to avoid.

The attempt to specify and order content units of a syllabus so as to correspond with natural learning, then, runs into problems for which we have (at present at least) no solutions, whether these units are defined in linguistic or non-linguistic terms. So if all syllabuses constitute an unnatural confinement which impedes the intuitive process of learning, why not accept the view previously mentioned and dispense with them altogether, letting courses develop out of classroom activity under their own momentum as a function of communicative interaction? But there are problems here too.

The limitations of intuitive learning

The belief that learning is best achieved by the unconstrained exercise of natural intuition would appear to be based on two related assumptions which, if not false, are certainly unfounded. I have already referred to these assumptions in Part 1 of this book. The first is that the operation of this natural intuition is necessarily made less effective by being constrained. The second assumption is that natural learning is necessarily more effective than learning that is induced by artifice. On closer examination both of these assumptions turn out to be of doubtful validity.

Against the first assumption one can argue that, unless one takes an extreme deterministic position, the very process of learning depends on the presence of constraints of one sort of another. Indeed, learning would seem to be of its nature a matter of accommodating intuitions to patterns of belief and behaviour established by convention. Learning, one might argue, is essentially an implied act of social conformity. This does not mean, of course, that there is no room for individual manoeuvre, for creativity, for the working of the imagination beyond the bounds of convention, but all of this presupposes the existence of such bounds. No freedom is possible unless there are limits to define it. So the constraints on learning are in effect the essential conditions of its existence. The child, for example, learns its mother tongue in the process of socialization, in the process, that is to say, of recognizing the limits to individual initiative defined by the conventional structures of its society. The child is not a free agent. If it were, it would learn nothing. So to speak of unconstrained learning, is really a contradiction in terms. The question is not how to set the learner free from constraints but what kind of constraints are likely to promote learning most effectively, and most likely, therefore, to provide eventual freedom of action. In this view it makes no sense to talk about dispensing with the syllabus, or of conceiving of it as a retrospective record because this simply denies the very nature of learning. Far from removing an impediment, it actually imposes one. We cannot avoid the responsibility of specifying and ordering content in advance in a syllabus. The question is: how can its design be made (in computer parlance) learner-friendly?

The second assumption underlying the belief in intuitive learning is that what is natural is self-evidently to be favoured as intrinsically good and desirable. This is a notion that has always had a powerful sentimental appeal. It would seem to arise from a longing for primitive innocence. But civilizations are based on a denial of its truth. They seek to improve on nature by artifice, and they are created on the contrary assumption that nature can be controlled, crafted, adapted, and fashioned into more manageable and convenient form. The assumption here is that what is natural is inchoate and inefficient compared with what can be contrived by the conscious application of human reason.

It seems to me that education, one of civilization's essential services, is similarly based on a belief in contrivance. Its business is not to defer to natural intuition but to direct it by ingenuity so that it is effectively applied in the acquisition of knowledge and ability. This does not mean that learners are thereby committed for life to strict confinement within the conventional constraints that serve the process of learning. Once knowledge and ability are acquired they can be turned against the conventions which brought them into being. But unless the learner first acquires these capabilities by accepting such conventions he is powerless to challenge them. Education in this way can provide for equal opportunity in a way that nature most assuredly does not.

Teaching, in this view, seeks to remedy by artifice the deficiencies of natural processes, and induce development which would otherwise be left to the vagaries of chance. In the case of second language learning, the process is inefficient in the normal circumstances of untutored acquisition, so it seems to be a perversion of pedagogy to seek to replicate these in the classroom. This does not, of course, mean that the particular characteristics of learners are to be deliberately disregarded. The artifice has to be such as to engage their interest and be consistent with their cognitive and affective dispositions. Artifice, like art itself, has to carry conviction.

The rejection of a syllabus as a projected programme of work for the teacher to follow in favour of allowing learning to happen by natural instinct is, in effect, to deny learners the necessary conditions for learning, and this is all the more pernicious when such denial is imposed by invoking the principle of individual freedom.

Apart from (but related to) the point that there needs to be some framework for learning, there is a second positive effect of the delimitation provided by a syllabus. This has to do not with the process of learning but with the well-being of the learner. A syllabus offers security. We return here to the suggestion I made at the beginning of this chapter that the general purpose of education is to initiate people into a secondary culture. This means that they are drawn away from a sole reliance on the patterns of familiar experience, and the more removed the secondary culture is from the primary, the greater the danger of alienation, and the loss of confidence and self-esteem. In such a situation, it is natural for learners to seek the solidarity of their peers and set up a counter-culture to that of the classroom. But if they are to be induced into formal learning they are likely to need some definite direction which will indicate the paths they are to follow, something known in advance, some frame of reference. This is what the syllabus can provide. No doubt there are some people who need no such guidance, who can plot their own course without worrying about losing their way. But many, it would appear, because of cultural or personal disposition, need the support which a projected plan of work can provide.

So the very nature of the educational enterprise, the very

purpose of the promotion of learning, would seem to require the design of an informing framework within which classroom activities can operate and in terms of which they take on significance. The syllabus provides the teacher with the basis for such a framework. How it is to be made operational as a particular course of instruction, and how instruction is itself to be defined, are methodological matters which are the concern of individual teachers. But to dispense with the syllabus is an act of self-inflicted disablement.

Criteria for syllabus design

If we are to accept the need of a syllabus, then by reference to what criteria is it to be designed? Criteria relating to the natural learning process, as might be revealed by research on second language acquisition, are not self-evidently relevant, even if they were available. It is of interest to note that in a recent paper one of the most authoritative figures in the SLA field, in considering the relevance of such research for syllabus design, can only conclude by putting forward proposals for task-based teaching (Long 1985). This, one has to say, is rather a small pedagogic return on such an extensive investment of research effort.

Enquiries are now increasingly being directed at the effect of classroom instruction on what is assumed to be the natural acquisition process (see Ellis 1985: Chapter 9; Long 1983c). This would seem logically to involve a convergence of SLA research with that which has been carried out on classroom interaction (see Seliger and Long 1983; Mitchell 1985) Færch and Kasper 1985; Allwright 1988; van Lier 1988), although curiously, Ellis deals with these areas of research in two quite separate chapters (1985: Chapters 6 and 9).

Insights may well emerge from such a convergence (as they may from the relationship mentioned earlier between SLA and LSP), but the variables involved in any consideration of different pedagogic practices have proved in the past to be so diverse and elusive that it is not easy to imagine at the moment what reliable guidance such insights might afford. The key notion of *instruction* itself has not so far in SLA research been subjected to much conceptual analysis and tends to be dealt with (as do other key concepts like communication and comprehension) in a quantitative and rather simplistic way (how much instruction rather than what kind). It is not easy to see how the shift to a more valid qualitative enquiry can retain reliability and so avoid the sort of difficulties encountered in, for example, the Pennsylvania Project (Smith 1970) in seeking to evaluate the effects of different kinds of classroom encounters; or the sort of rather inconsequential proliferation of learner characteristics coming out of research on the 'Good Language Learner' (see Naiman *et al.* 1978; Rubin 1975, 1981; Stern 1983). It is not easy to see either, in the light of the observations made earlier, how any findings (no matter how suggestive for methodology) would have any direct bearing on syllabus design as such.

Meanwhile, what are we to do? On the one hand we need the syllabus to give shape to instruction (however conceived) but on the other hand we do not seem to have any definite or authoritative guidance as to how to set about its design. Neither goal-oriented criteria which relate to proficiency nor process-oriented criteria which relate to achievement seem to be satisfactory, whether these are applied to the specification of syllabus content or to the manner of its arrangement. And I think it is unlikely that any research at present or in the future will provide us with anything very definite to resolve these difficulties.

But then I am not sure that this matters very much. For I am not convinced that the issue of just how the content of a syllabus should be specified and arranged is actually a very crucial one. To my mind, what is crucial is that the principles upon which the syllabus has been designed, whether in terms of structures, notions, functions, topics, or tasks, should be made quite explicit so that teachers can submit them to appraisal and application. In this way they can make use of the syllabus as a set of bearings for the plotting of their own course in a lesson sequence, and for the realization of aspects of language and learning which the syllabus of its nature cannot account for. Conceived of in this fashion, a syllabus is a rationalized construct whose principles of design are made plain so that teachers can refer to them, and not just to the design itself, to make their own methodological plans to suit the circumstances of their particular classroom. In this explicit, explanatory form, the syllabus becomes an important element in the continuing education of teachers as they experiment with its variable realization in the process of actual teaching (see Chapter 3). And such a conception of the syllabus acknowledges that although learners must ultimately accept individual responsibility for their own learning, it is the teacher who must, as social agent, prepare them for this responsibility by setting the limits which condition learning. And she cannot do this unless she herself has limits within which she can define her own enterprise and it is these which it is the essential purpose of the syllabus to provide.

10 Methodology for the teaching of meaning

Structural and communicative approaches: knowing and doing

It follows from the characterization of language proposed in the preceding part of this book that learning a language as a natural human accomplishment involves getting to *know* something, and being able to *do* something with that knowledge. Language learning has two sides to it: knowing and doing (competence and performance), the first associated with a medium and the second with a mediation perspective on meaning, as these are defined in the introductory chapter of this section. And as I pointed out there, different approaches to language teaching have tended to emphasize one rather than, and often at the expense of, the other.

Thus the approach to language teaching in fashion until the recent past, the so-called 'structural approach', focuses attention on knowing. Here items of language, words and sentences, are presented and practised in a way which is intended best to help the learners to internalize them as forms containing meaning within themselves, as semantic capsules, so to speak. The assumption is that once learners have achieved this semantic knowledge, then they will be able to use it pragmatically to do things: to converse, to read, to write; to engage, in short, in communicative activity of the same kind (if not to the same degree) as that associated with their mother tongue. The assumption is, generally speaking, that the primary task of teaching is to impart knowledge and that the learners can be left to find out how to do things with it for themselves.

This does not mean that classrooms where this approach is followed are devoid of activity. Typically there is a great deal of doing: learners speaking in pairs and in groups, reading passages, composing sentences, busy practising the four skills.

But in this approach, these activities are seen essentially as a means to the internalization of knowledge and not as ends which are achieved by the use of knowledge. Their purpose is to stimulate participation in the use of skills to help in learning the language system as a medium for meaning. They differ therefore from the kind of doings which we would associate with normal uses of language, where the purpose is to achieve some outcome outside language learning and where linguistic knowledge is drawn upon as a means and not an end, as a frame of reference for the mediation of meaning.

Let me dwell on this point for a moment, because it seems to me to be an important one. In the approach I am talking about— the structural approach—the activities which call for the exercise of different skills are designed to help the learners to consolidate their knowledge of language. They are devices which are designed to service language learning. The doing is subservient to knowing. But of course in the usual business of language *using*, you do not go around speaking sentences in order to practise them, or reading passages of prose in order to get more exposure to particular structural patterns. In normal language use, in normal activity with language, we always have some purpose which language is there to serve. The knowing is subservient to doing.

It has been pointed out often enough in recent years that the disadvantage of this structural approach is that it does not allow the learners to use language in a natural way. They tend to fixate on form for its own sake, internalize the language system as a separate body of knowledge and fail to learn for themselves how to use it. Having been trained to direct what they do in the service of knowing, they have difficulty in reversing the dependency and so to direct what they know in the service of doing. This is not surprising. For the structural approach requires the learners to conceive of the foreign language as something very different from their mother tongue, something designed as a subject with its own rules for learning which seem to have very little in common with the learner's own experience of language. For their own experience will have been in using language in the mediation of meaning for some purposeful outcome and not in the contemplation of the formal and semantic properties of the medium itself.

The principles of structural language teaching, then, seem to be at variance with the natural use of language which it is the purpose of such teaching to promote as the eventual aim of learning. The structural *means of teaching* would appear to be inconsistent with the communicative *ends of learning*. This paradox can be resolved, in practice, by the dominance of teaching so that in effect learners do not learn how to do communicative things with what they have acquired as knowledge, but simply learn how to display their knowledge according to conventions established by teaching and to meet the requirements of the examinations based on the same conventions. These are traditionally designed to test a knowledge of the subject itself as defined by the language teachers, and not what learners have learned to do by means of the subject. Thus such examinations are based on the norm of what has been taught, not the criterion of what needs to be learnt.

One way of resolving the paradox, then, is to retain the structural approach principle and make practice conform to it. Another way is to adopt a different principle, indeed a directly opposite principle, and make the means of teaching conform to the communicative ends of learning. We adopt, in other words, a communicative approach to language teaching and concentrate on doing.

The communicative approach reverses the emphasis of the structural. It concentrates on getting learners to do things with language, to express concepts and to carry out communicative acts of various kinds. The content of a language course is now defined not in terms of forms, words and sentence patterns, but in terms of the concepts, or notions, which such forms are used to express, and the communicative functions which they are used to perform. Hence the notional/functional syllabus. But, as I argued in Chapter 9, this definition of course content is not enough to ensure that there is an emphasis on doing in the language classroom. There also needs to be a methodology which will implement this course content in such a way that learners will be activated to realize the notional and functional character of the course specification. It is perfectly possible to treat notions and functions as items to be learned in the same way as structures, as pieces of knowledge to be put in store without any necessary implication for actual use as natural behaviour. If a methodology, a set of classroom techniques, is focused on teaching knowledge in the abstract, and directs all learner activity to that end, then it will fail to realize the communicative possibilities within a notional/functional syllabus. It will indeed convert such a syllabus into what to all intents and purposes is a structural one. The notional/functional syllabus only becomes 'communicative' when it is implemented by appropriate methodology.

A crucial element of the communicative approach to language teaching is the adoption of a methodology which will encourage learners to do things with the language they are learning, the kind of things they will recognize as purposeful and communicative and have some resemblance to what they use their own language to do. The assumption is that if the learners use the language in this way, then they will learn it contingently, as a natural consequence, that knowing will emerge from doing. In other words, what teaching is concerned with is setting up conditions for effective performance with the language on the assumption that in learning how to perform pragmatically learners will somehow be able to acquire knowledge of the language itself inferentially by themselves.

So we have two approaches characterized by different emphases. The principles, put simply, amount to this. The structural approach is based on the belief that language learning comes about by teaching learners to know the forms of the language as a medium and the meaning they incorporate; that they will learn how to do things with this knowledge on their own. The communicative approach is based on the contrary belief that language learning comes about when the teacher gets learners to use the language pragmatically to mediate meanings for a purpose, to do things which resemble in some measure what they do with their own language. They will learn a knowledge of the language itself, the formal and semantic properties of the medium, as they go along, without the teacher having to draw explicit attention to it.

It is of course the communicative approach which is in current fashion. It is not difficult to see why its principles should be so appealing. They bring the means of learning into alignment with its eventual ends—the achievement of an ability to use language to communicative effect. Furthermore, at the same time, they represent the language to be learned as the same sort of natural phenomenon as the language the learners already know, and so allow them to draw on their own experience in the process of learning. This in turn means that the focus of attention shifts to the learner, who becomes the dominant partner in the pedagogic enterprise so that instead of having the assertive teacher dictating to the submissive learner, we have the teacher submissive to the requirements that assert themselves as necessary for successful learning. I shall take up this question of the roles of teacher and learner in more detail in Chapter 11.

So the communicative approach seems not only to be more natural and less contrived, but also seems to have the added advantage of providing for the human rights of learners. So on both pedagogic and democratic grounds it might seem self-evidently preferable to the structural approach. A happy coincidence of good causes, one might think: the learners achieve their language learning objectives as a function of increased independence, under the benevolent guidance or counsel of the teacher, who is no longer the autocratic controller of their destiny.

The problems of a communicative approach

Such an approach has its obvious attractions. Unfortunately, it also has its problems, as I indicated earlier in this book (see particularly Chapters 3 and 8). Two might be mentioned of specific relevance to the present discussion. One of them has to do with natural language *learning* and the other with natural language *use*.

The natural *learning* problem is this. It turns out that learners do not very readily infer knowledge of the language system from their communicative activities. The grammar, which they must obviously acquire somehow as a necessary resource for use, proves elusive. So quite often the situation arises where learners acquire a fairly patchy and imperfect repertoire of performance which is not supported by an underlying competence. Their doing does not seem to lead naturally to knowing, as has been optimistically assumed.

The reason for this can be inferred from the characterization of language use presented in the chapters in Part 2. As I observed there, in using language we quite naturally follow the principle of communicative economy whereby we pay attention to linguistic features only to the extent needed to make connection with context and so achieve the indexical meaning suited to our purpose. This process of mediation does not depend on linguistic analysis. On the contrary, it will often involve the matching up and adjustment to context of pre-assembled patterns of language of the sort discussed in Chapter 6. Some adjustment might be needed, but not analysis. Indeed, analysis would in many instances be out of place and disruptive. So the process of communication which calls for external synthesis with context would run counter to the process needed to develop competence, which calls for the internal analysis of the language itself. Thus the conditions favourable for establishing external relations necessary for effective use are different from the conditions favourable for establishing internal relations necessary for effective learning.

But it might be objected that these conditions are not in fact different in the natural development of first language acquisition. This is true, but irrelevant. The natural language acquisition process is a long and rather inefficient business. For the child acquiring its mother tongue, knowing a language and internalizing its formal rules is something that happens gradually through trial and error; its competence is the result of a recurrent refocusing as required by increasing performance demands over a period of extensive exposure to and experience of language. Courses for the teaching of other languages in schools just cannot provide such conditions for natural learning.

Nor does it make any sense to try. For the whole point of pedagogy is that it is a way of short-circuiting the slow process of natural discovery and can make arrangements for learning to happen more easily and more efficiently than it does in 'natural surroundings'. This is what schools are for, whatever subject we are dealing with. Pedagogy is bound to be a contrivance: that is precisely its purpose. If what went on in classrooms exactly replicated the conditions of the world outside, there would be no point in pedagogy at all. And, in respect of the present argument, the advantage of pedagogy is denied if it just leaves learners to learn by doing without quite deliberately contriving ways of assisting them in getting to know the language system at the same time, as the essential resource for their doings.

Put simply, the problem connected with natural language *use* is this. As I pointed out in Chapter 7, when using language indexically either to convey our intended meaning, or to interpret the meanings of other people, we adopt strategies of differential access and analysis in the interests of effective communication. We do not derive meaning from a close consideration or analysis of the language itself, we bypass it if we can, treating it rather cavalierly as a set of clues which we can follow in order to discover meanings elsewhere. When language is used it becomes a set of pointers which indicate what area of knowledge of the world must be brought to mind for interpretation to be achieved. In other words, we do not find meaning in the medium, we achieve it by mediation.

For example, when we read the newspaper in the ordinary course of everyday life, we do not submit the language to close scrutiny, carefully deciphering every word and sentence to extract its meaning. The language provides us with access to what we already know, it indicates to us what already existing knowledge we need to engage as a frame of reference into which any new information might be fitted. It is only when we cannot engage a frame of reference that we focus attention on the language itself. So when we come across a word we do not know, we do not immediately reach for the dictionary, we pass over it, assuming that we will be able to fit it into the framework subsequently by inference. Only when we fail to make the fit, when a word does not activate our knowledge, do we begin to enquire into its specific meaning.

To recapitulate the arguments of Chapters 5–7, natural language use in the expressing and interpretation of meanings is only in part a matter of language. The process involves taking bearings, as it were, on two kinds of knowledge. One of these is indeed knowledge of the formal properties of language, its semantics and syntax, the meanings of words and their combination in sentences, a knowledge of the properties of the medium, *systemic knowledge*. The other kind of knowledge is that which we have of the particular world we live in, our beliefs, ideas, experiences, cultural values, and so on, *schematic knowledge*. The meanings we achieve through the use of language, whether we are sending or receiving them, are a function of a dual reference to these two kinds of knowledge.

But in natural language use, as we have seen, systemic knowledge is subservient to the schematic. It is a means to the achievement of meaning and not an end in itself. And when we are using language to deal with what is familiar to us as we normally do, we pay as little attention to language as possible. But when we do encounter unfamiliar content, or when we want to express ideas which are novel and which do not fit conventional schematic patterns, we, as native speakers, have systemic knowledge to fall back on. We can use this as a communicative resource.

Here then is the essential problem about natural language use for language learning. We do not want our learners to bypass language when they use it, as it is natural for native speakers to do, because they do not have the systemic knowledge as a back-up resource to rely on. This is precisely what we want them to acquire and it is the purpose of pedagogy to assist them in acquiring it.

Let me summarize the points I have made against a too-ready acceptance of the primacy of doing. To try to replicate the conditions of natural communicative use of language in class-rooms is mistaken for two basic reasons. First, to do so is to deny the whole purpose of pedagogy, which is to contrive economical and more effective means for language learning than is provided by natural exposure and experience. Second, natural language use typically deflects attention from language itself and pre-supposes a knowledge of the language system as a basic resource which learners have, by definition, not yet acquired.

Reconciling the oppositions: an illustration

It would appear that a strict adherence to neither structural nor communicative principles of approach, as I have outlined them here, will provide satisfactorily for the interplay between knowing and doing upon which (I have argued) effective language use and language learning depend. We need to reconcile these contraries by methodological procedures which draw on both approaches and realize the necessary interdepend-ence of knowledge and behaviour.

This is not, of course, a new discovery. Many teachers recognize this need for reconciliation well enough. The profes-sion of language teaching is not neatly divided into groups of teachers who adhere strictly to one approach or the other. All distinctions of the kind I am making here are based on an idealization, an abstraction of salient features, and are con-founded in reality. The two approaches I have outlined are modified and combined in different ways under the influence of varying circumstances. In other words, they are expediently applied. So there are already methodological compromises to be found in existing teaching materials and in the practices of individual teachers which can be said to bring about the reconciliation that I refer to. What I want to do now is to illustrate this process of reconciliation by reference to a particular exercise in materials design. My purpose is to demonstrate how the specific techniques proposed derive from a consideration of general principles. The demonstration, therefore, is an example of the pragmatics of language pedagogy discussed in the first part of this book: having subjected ideas to critical appraisal, we now move on to make them operational.

The illustration is a set of communicative grammar materials originally designed to complement a course which had been written along notional/functional lines for the Arab World.[1] This course was based essentially on the assumption which has already been referred to—that knowing will be derived from doing by natural inference without direct intervention in the form of explicit demonstration or conscious practice.

Grammar, then, was to be assimilated incidentally as a function of communicative activity. One difficulty with this approach to methodology relates to points I mentioned at the beginning of Chapter 9: pedagogically enlightened though it may seem to be, such an approach is not closely congruent with the educational context. Both teachers and learners were accustomed to an approach in which explicit grammatical directions were provided. The new course required learners to shift from a referential to an inferential mode of learning (from referring to knowledge in doing things to inferring knowledge from doing things) and this led to some degree of disorientation. And it turned out that the learners could not always discover their own grammatical bearings by generalizing from particular instances of behaviour. Grammatical knowledge did not always follow as a necessary corollary of communication. The learners, in short, and the teachers too, needed some sort of chart which marked out the grammatical features of the learning terrain to help them to find their way. This is what these communicative grammar materials set out to provide.

---

[1] The course which these materials were designed to complement is the *Crescent* English course. The materials themselves were published under the title of *Communicative Grammar*, the first four books of which were written by Ann Brumfit and Scott Windeatt and the last two books by Christopher Hyde. Both the main *Crescent* course and *Communicative Grammar* appear under the imprint of ELTA/OUP (English Language Teaching for the Arab World/Oxford University Press) Beirut.

It should be noted that the *Crescent* course has been subject to recurrent revision over the years in the light of teachers' experience in using it and in consequence there has been a more focused attention to the formal properties of language in later editions. The development of this course from its early conception to its most recent revision is an interesting case history of the relationship between pedagogic ideas and the educational context which sets conditions for their implementation (see Chapter 8).

What they did was to reformulate the grammar which appeared informally and contingently in the main course. This involved the selection of those elements of grammar which seemed to call for focal treatment (leaving the rest to be inferred from peripheral use) and the design of units of work which would draw attention to the aspects of conceptual and communicative meaning which these elements encoded as semantically intrinsic in their forms (that is to say, their denotation), and also to the relationship these elements contracted with others as terms within the linguistic systems of English (that is to say, their sense relations).

But simply to take language originally presented as a kind of communicative scatter and reformulate it explicitly as grammar, even though tagged with notional/functional values, would clearly have run the risk of presenting it as an area of knowledge in detachment from its communicative realization. It would not have provided the necessary transitional dependency between knowing and doing. Grammar had to be internalized not just as a formal system but as a resource for use. This meant that activities needed to be devised which would require learners to access grammatical knowledge for some purpose other than practice and so to realize for themselves the latent capability within grammatical knowledge for the achievement of meaning. In other words, the activities would need to establish the relevance of systemic knowledge and the credentials of the medium as a crucial factor in the realization of meaning by mediation.

The procedure was first to demonstrate how grammatical forms typically correlate with areas of meaning and then to involve learners in problem-solving tasks whereby they could put these forms to purposeful use. An example of the demonstration stage appears in Figure 3.

Two features of this demonstration call for comment. First, the little diagrammatic device at the beginning is intended to represent the conceptual meaning of the particular grammatical form. This 'grammargraph' (as it was called) is a mnemonic device which indicates by non-verbal symbolism both the standard or core denotation of the form and, by contrast with other grammargraphs, the sense relations it contracts with other forms as terms within the grammatical systems concerned. Thus, this particular grammargraph clearly contrasts with others, shown

Figure 3

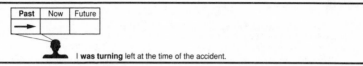

I **was turning** left at the time of the accident.

7   Whose fault was it?

7.1   **Which car is Fuad's, and which is Ahmed's?**
Read the sentences and look at the map to find out.
Then write the names in the correct boxes.

This morning Fuad was driving along South
Street while Ahmed was driving along West
Street. At 10.01 they had an accident at the
crossroads.

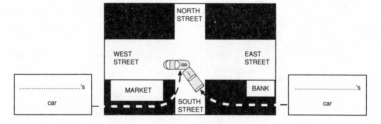

7.2   Ahmed and Fuad told the police about the accident. They
both told the truth. What were they doing at the time of the
accident? Were they turning left or right? Was one of them
driving carelessly? Read the passages to find out, and then
tick the correct boxes for the sentences below.

Ahmed
'At 10.00 I was driving along West Street. I was
going to the bank. I was watching the traffic
lights and while I was driving past the market,
they changed to green. The other car was
turning left out of South Street when it hit my
car. I was not going very fast.'

Fuad
'At 10.00 I was driving along South Street with
my friend, Ali. We were going to the market
and we were not going very fast. We were
talking when the accident happened.'

	True	Untrue
1 Fuad was turning left.		
2 Ahmed was turning right.		
3 Fuad and Ali were talking.		
4 Ahmed and Fuad were not going very fast.		

(continued)

PAST TIME

7.3   **So whose fault was it? Who was driving carelessly when the accident happened? Complete the passage.**

Ahmed and Fuad .... very fast, but .... was driving carelessly. The

accident was ....'s fault. He .... left into ....Street when

the traffic lights in .... Street were red.

7.4   **Complete the tables.**

| At the time of the accident, | he she it I | was | .... the traffic lights. |
| | we you they | .... | .... to the market. |

| At the time of the accident, | he she it I | .... | .... | .... very fast. |
| | we you they | .... | | |

| At the time of the accident, | .... | he she it I | .... carelessly? |
| | .... | we you they | .... left or right? |

in Figure 4, which represent the simple past, the present continuous, and the present perfect. How far the kind of symbolic representation exemplified by these grammargraphs is effective in teaching conceptual meaning is an open question. Some areas of meaning clearly lend themselves more naturally to such representation than do others.

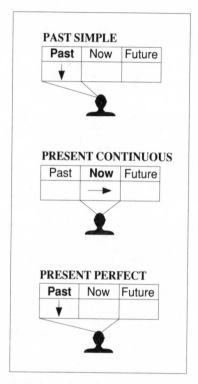

Figure 4

Spatial prepositions, for example, are straightforward enough. Figure 5 (overleaf) shows a set of grammargraphs, which represent motion and position in the second book of *Communicative Grammar* (see also Quirk *et al.* 1972: 307).

Things get more difficult, however, the more remote meanings become from immediate perceptual experience. Here one relies on the learner acquiring the conventions which are established by the devices themselves. But there can be problems even with concepts which seem simple because they are more or less directly derivable from the perceived world. Take the notion of

MOTION AND POSITION

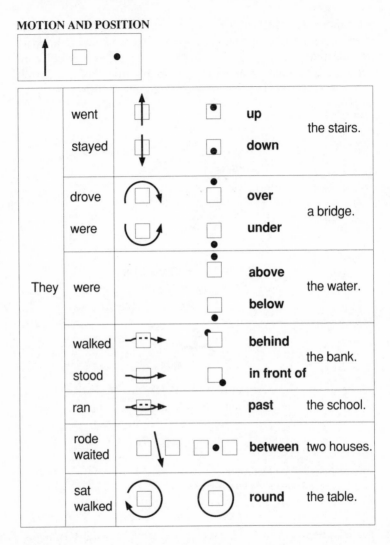

Figure 5

relative proximity (*near/far, here/there, this/that*, etc.). An obvious way of symbolizing this would be to show two figures, one in the foreground, the other in the background. But a correct interpretation depends on a familiarity with the convention of perspective drawing. Otherwise the figures could be read as representing relative size. It has to be remembered, then, that pictorial and diagrammatical devices are based on cultural convention just as linguistic devices are.

Nevertheless, for all this, it seems worth pursuing the possibilities of grammargraphs of this kind. For one thing, they can be particularly useful in demonstrating the abstract sense relations that hold between grammatical elements, the way in which they contrast with each other as terms within a system. They can also be used as frames of reference for establishing the differences between the mother tongue and the language being learned in respect to the manner in which reality is encoded.

The second feature of the demonstration to be noted is that the learners are not cast in the role of passive recipients of information. They are drawn into participation through the solving of a simple problem which requires the repetitive use of the form in question. This leads to the completion of a substitution table of the conventional kind which formalizes the knowledge they have derived from the preceding activity and serves as a source of reference for subsequent use. There is provision for doing, then, in this demonstration stage, but it is doing at the service of knowing, a variant of conventional form-focused activity.

The demonstration stage seeks to establish the standard or canonical notional/functional valency of the linguistic forms, their prototypical value as it were. In the tasks which follow, learners are required to act on this information through activities which provide an opportunity for repeated use of these forms, but as motivated by a problem-solving purpose. Here the dependency of language and task is reversed: knowing is put at the service of doing. The outcome is a solution and not a substitution table.

An example of a problem-solving activity which follows on from the given demonstration appears as Figure 6 (pages 174–5).

The relationship between the demonstration stage and the problem solving that follows it is in some respects similar to the relationship between pre-task and task in Prabhu's procedural approach to teaching. In both cases, the first activity primes the learner for the second. The difference is that the priming in Prabhu's case is not explicitly linguistic:

The pre-task is a context in which any difficulties which learners may have in understanding the nature of the activity —seeing what information is given, what needs to be done, and what constraints apply—are revealed and the teacher is

able to provide appropriate assistance, perhaps by paraphrasing or glossing expressions, by employing parallel
situations or diagrams, or by re-organizing information. In
this sense, the pre-task is preparation for the task, since
learners are less likely, while engaged later in a similar activity
on their own, to fail to see what is given and what needs to be
done. *(1987: 54)*

I do not myself see why explicit reference to language should
be so stringently avoided in preparation for the task. Linguistic
information and linguistic constraints are just as much a part of
the nature of the activity as anything else. And in practice, the
learners are indeed given linguistic instruction in the pre-task by
means of 'paraphrasing and glossing expressions'.

Apart from providing learners with linguistic priming, the
demonstration stage also, like Prabhu's pre-task, prepares the
learners to engage in a particular kind of problem-solving
activity—so it seeks to establish a close relationship between
language and reasoning. In the demonstration stage it is the
latter which is the dependent partner and in the stage which
follows, the dependency is reversed. In Prabhu's scheme, the
reasoning is always given primary emphasis.

Of course, the crucial condition on this reversal of dependency
is that learners will engage with the tasks as purposeful problem-
solving activities and not as linguistic exercises. The tasks have
to be such as to seem worthwhile in their own right and
independently motivating. And they of course also have to be
within the conceptual scope of the learners. Here we encounter a
general difficulty with reasoning-gap activities, one that was
touched upon in Chapter 9, namely that we have no reliable
measure of their relative complexity. Complexity, furthermore,
may be culturally variable. What is a familiar mode of reasoning
in one culture may not be familiar at all in another. It should also
be noted that too great a reliance on reasoning might preclude
the learner from engaging more affectively with the language,
might narrow the scope for imaginative and emotional involvement. Prabhu has countered this argument by making a
distinction between learning and teaching. He acknowledges
that his tasks are factual and rational in meaning-content and
that they require no procedures for increasing emotional
involvement, but adds: 'This does not imply any denial of value
to emotional involvement in *learning*. What it implies is a

recognition of the much greater suitability of rational activity for language *teaching*.' (1987: 52)

In other words, emotional involvement is seen as an incidental and contingent effect of teacher-directed reasoning. In this respect it seems to resemble the acquisition of grammatical competence itself in Prabhu's scheme of things. But letting emotional involvement happen (by connivance almost) is very different from encouraging it actively as a matter of positive pedagogic policy as in humanistic approaches to language teaching (for example, Asher 1982; Moskowitz 1978; Rogers 1969). In such approaches, indeed, such a distinction between learning and teaching is hardly tenable.

The fact remains that reasoning-gap activities in Prabhu's approach, and in the communicative grammar materials presented in this chapter are, in the terms I used earlier (Chapter 2), designed for cognitive regulation, and they do restrict the engagement of the learners' personality in a way which proponents of humanistic learning, who believe in affective regulation, would find unacceptable. It should be noted, however, that these communicative grammar tasks are designed to be complementary, so that they do allow for the possibility of learner personality to be more extensively and affectively engaged elsewhere in other parts of the programme. I will return to this point later in the chapter.

It should be stressed that the problems which are posed in these tasks are not language problems but problems which require a use of language for their solution. The learners do not just manipulate language as an end in itself, but realize its potential as a means for achieving outcomes which have independent point. The design of the problems, therefore, seems to reconcile two features which are commonly associated with two different approaches to the teaching of language: linguistic repetition, with its necessary focus on form, and non-linguistic purpose, with its necessary focus on meaning. Linguistic repetition is a feature of a structural orientation to teaching with its emphasis on knowing: learners are required to practise particular structures so as to facilitate unconscious assimilation. Non-linguistic purpose is a feature of a communicative orientation with its emphasis on doing: here learners are engaged in activities which deflect attention away from the linguistic forms being used. But in these communicative grammar materials, the tasks are so designed that their solution depends on the repeated

PAST TIME

8   What were they doing at 11.00?

At 11.00 yesterday morning, a thief took a box
of watches from Salim's watch shop. A
policeman arrived, and stopped seven people
near the shop. He asked each of them: 'What
were you doing at 11.00?'
The policeman wrote down their answers in
shorthand, because he wanted to write quickly.

8.1   **Look at the policeman's notebook. What did he write?**
Use the key for the shorthand words and the map below to find out.

POLICEMAN'S NOTEBOOK

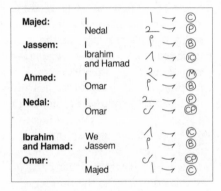

KEY FOR THE SHORTHAND WORDS

THE MAP

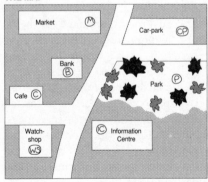

Figure 6

8.2 What were the seven people doing at 11.00? Use the
policeman's notebook to complete everybody's answers.
The thief told *two lies*, and everybody else told the truth.
So if two people said the same thing, it was true.

Majed: I......*was eating*...... in the .*cafe*............... .

Nedal.. in the ......*park*........ .

Jassem: I................................... in the .*bank*............... .

Ibrahim and Hamad .... in the

....

Ahmed: I................................. in the ....

Omar................................. in the ....

Nedal: I................................. in the ....

Omar................................. in the ....

Ibrahim
& Hamad: We................................. in the ....

Jassem................................. in the ....

Omar: I................................. in the ....

Majed................................. in the ....

8.3 Who told the lies? Read the sentences in 8.2 again to find out.
Then write everybody's names in the boxes round the map,
and draw lines to show where everybody was.
Who was in the watch-shop?

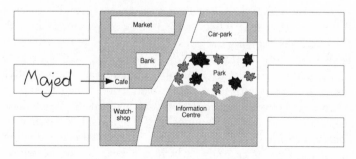

.................................told two lies, so he was the thief.

use of the language items concerned: repetition, therefore, is a function of purpose. The learner practises language in the process of solving the non-linguistic problem. There is no conflict between form and meaning: the one complements the other.

This accommodation of the two cardinal principles of repetition and purpose, which in combination provide for the internalization of grammar as a resource for use, places constraints of course on the design of the tasks themselves. In particular, they operate at a remove from verisimilitude of the simulation of the real world. An attempt to use scenes and events from everyday life (favoured as typically communicative in other teaching materials) would have resulted in distortion after the manner of a structural approach in order to provide for the required repetition of linguistic forms, and this would inevitably have involved a corresponding reduction in communicative point. Neither the problem to be solved nor the language needed to solve it could have been so sharply focused. The procedure, therefore, was to devise problems whose very purpose lay in contrivance, which sought to create their own contexts of significance and which in this respect bear a closer resemblance to what learners are required to do in other subjects on the curriculum than to naturalistic uses of language in the social world outside the classroom.

There are two further points of principle implicit in this design feature of the tasks. First, the approach to language teaching is brought into closer alignment with activities associated with other areas of school work and allows for the possibility of integration within the curriculum as a whole. Secondly, there is the implication that what the learners are acquiring through these problem-solving tasks is not primarily a repertoire of behaviour ready for direct deployment but a capacity for actual use based on the internalization of grammar as a communicative resource. This point relates to the distinction which I made in Chapter 9 between accumulation and investment. What these materials aim to bring about is not a rehearsal of 'authentic' communication in the sense of naturalistic social behaviour but an investment in grammar which has been authenticated as meaning potential by having been realized through these tasks in the achievement of purposeful outcomes.

Further developments: text sequences

I should make it clear that I am not suggesting that methodology should consist entirely of an unrelieved diet of this sort of communicative grammar. These tasks should be seen as complementary to activities which are less specifically focused on the medium, which allow for less controlled mediation of meaning and for the contingent learning of language. They could be complementary in two ways. They could provide a retrospective reformulation of elements of grammar which had been informally introduced in communicative guise in previous teaching. This was the purpose for which these particular materials were originally designed. But tasks of this kind can also be complementary in a prospective way: they can prepare the ground for problem solving as the negotiating process which (as I indicated in Chapter 7) defines language use in general. Thus one can envisage, for example, a development from these tasks in the form of work on texts which gradually shifted dependence from systemic to schematic knowledge and which required learners to negotiate interpretation by the discriminating reliance on both. In this way they would gradually approximate to 'natural' language behaviour by taking short cuts and adjusting their level of attention to language according to purpose. But they would previously have been provided with the basic systemic knowledge which is necessary as a back-up resource to be referred to when required.

Such a sequence of tasks would make increasing demands on procedures for negotiating meaning. Whereas the problem solving involved in the tasks of these communicative grammar materials has primary focus on the medium, and so relates more specifically to the matters discussed in Chapter 6, later texts would emphasize the procedures of mediation which are discussed in Chapter 7. Such a development would make operational the necessary interdependency of these two perspectives on methodology for the teaching of meaning.

One source of texts which are of particular interest here is literature. As I have argued elsewhere (for example, Widdowson 1984a: Section 4), in literature we find not *reference* to reality conventionally conceived but *representation* of alternative constructs of reality, not actual but possible worlds, existing in a different dimension. These cannot of their nature simply be recognized by calling up relevant schematic knowledge: they have to be realized through the language which creates them. Even when literature makes mention of objects, places, and events which are familiar, they have to be located in the created context of an imagined world which cannot be familiar, so their significance is never just a matter of recognition. The problem posed by a literary text is how to use systemic knowledge to gain access to a self-enclosed world that has no existence outside the text itself, and is not subject to normal standards of truth or rationality. The interpretation of literature, then, involves acts of schematic realignment and these can only be achieved by a particularly intensive exploitation of the language medium. And of course the literary writer encourages the reader in such exploitation. Consider, for example, the following opening of a short story by Somerset Maugham:

The Unconquered
He came back into the kitchen. The man was still on the floor, lying where he hit him, and his face was bloody. He was moaning. The woman had backed against the wall and was staring with terrified eyes at Willi, his friend, and when he came in she gave a gasp and broke into loud sobbing.

The use of the personal pronoun would normally signal shared knowledge. The pronoun would refer to some identifiable person. But here of course there is no person that the reader can recognize as referent for the pronoun that appears at the beginning of the passage. The reader is therefore drawn into the text and projected forward in quest of information as to who this person might be. And then another unidentified person appears: 'the woman'. Which woman? Who is she? Why is she so terrified? Why has the second man been hit by the first? Where has the first man come from? What has been happening here? The only way to find out is to pay close attention to the text: interpretative procedures are put, as it were, on special alert. And we read on, creating the fictional world by exploiting the language as we go along (see Widdowson 1985).

It is often suggested that learners should be primed to read texts by establishing a purpose for reading beforehand, by preparing them by means of a pre-task which is in effect a pretext. Obviously this can often be an effective strategy. But some texts, notably (though not exclusively) literary ones, are designed to attract attention and so provide their own priming.

Here contextual discovery can be encouraged in preference to pretextual preparation.

The point about literary uses of language is that communicative significance is realized as a function of a close attention to the language itself. As a further illustration, consider the following simple little poem by Emily Dickinson:

A word is dead
When it is said,
    Some say,

I say it just
Begins to live
    That day.

As before, we have no context that we can refer these expressions to. The words appear on the page as having some sort of self-enclosed significance—a significance which does not carry over in a prose paraphrase:

Some people say that once a word is said it is dead, but I say that it is only then that it begins to live.

This simply sounds banal and inconsequential. So there must be something in the particular choice of language arranged in this particular pattern which is meaningful. Without contextual connections, the only clues to significance must be contained within the language of the poem, inherent in those features of form which do not carry over into a conventional prose paraphrase which presupposes context. So we are drawn into the poem. What, then, might we infer from it?

Consider, for example, the way in which the propositions have been verbally fashioned. The predicate in the first line is stative: 'A word *is dead*'. That in the second line might be interpreted as a passive, but its parallel syntactic position and its phonological and metrical equivalence gives it stative force in association with the preceding line. A word is dead = a word is said. The two lines, we may say, thus indicate stasis, absence of movement. They do not only express the proposition 'a word is dead when it is said', they actually represent, in the very syntax, the identical state of 'deadness' and 'saidness'. In the second part of the poem, however, the verb in the predicate is dynamic, being active in voice and inceptive in aspect, so that the expression 'begins to live' can be said both to *refer* to birth and at the same time to *represent* it. This effect is furthermore enhanced by the simple and uninterrupted continuity of the syntactic pattern which carries the reader over line boundaries as if impelled by the elemental life-force itself.

The sense of the finality, the abrupt closure of death, in the first verse of the poem and the contrasting active and initiatory movement in the second verse are represented by syntactic and prosodic structuring and the meanings intrinsic to the grammar of the verb phrase. The death and life of words are in contrast, not only as they are expressed explicitly in the propositions, by virtue of lexical meaning, but also as they are implicitly represented in the form. What is said *about* words becomes indistinguishable from what is done *with* them. Their death is denied in their very use: they come alive as they are said as is evident from the interpretations they provoke.

Access to both the fictional world of character and event in the short story opening, and to the expression of experience in the poem depend, in different ways, on paying close attention to language. In both cases we find a kind of problem solving directed towards the realization of communicative significance. The meaning achieved is very different from that which comes from the cognitive tasks illustrated by the communicative grammar materials demonstrated in this chapter. For one thing, literary texts encourage a more affective engagement with language and so increase scope for personality involvement. But different though the meaning is, the point is that it too depends on a focus on language itself. Now, clearly, careful thought needs to be given to how literary texts should be selected and presented so that they are pedagogically effective. But it is not difficult to see how, in principle, such texts can be used, in association with others of a referential rather than representational kind, where the communicative purpose and reference to schematic knowledge call for less conscious concern with the systemic meanings intrinsic in language. Further discussion of the ways in which literature and language study can complement each other is to be found in Brumfit and Carter (1986) and Widdowson (1975, 1984a: Section 4, 1985).

So we can envisage a programme consisting of texts selected and presented in such a way as to require a differential and discriminating attention to systemic and schematic knowledge. The sequence would in effect gradually shift dependency on these two kinds of knowledge in the procedures for negotiating meaning.

11 The roles of teacher and learner

This book began with a consideration of the relationship between the roles of teacher and researcher. It ends with a consideration of the relationship between teacher and learner. Some aspects of this relationship have already been touched on in the preceding chapters. In particular I pointed out how a mediation-oriented methodology allows for the greater exercise of learner initiative, with the consequent modifications of directive control on the part of the teacher. But although one might commend this redefinition of relationship, whereby learners are able to participate more fully and freely in the development of their own learning, there are certain constraining factors in force. One has to do with the fact that all learning must be delimited in some way as a consideration of its happening at all (I discussed this matter in Chapter 1). Other factors have to do with the nature of teacher and learner roles in general, with what might be called the sociology of the classroom. These are the factors I shall be concerned with in this chapter.

Types of role

The term 'role' is a familiar one and frequent use has worn away its foreign circumflex. It can be defined, generally, as a part people play in the performance of social life. Roles, whether achieved or ascribed, are kinds of conventional script, or pre-script, which constrain the individual person to assume a persona in conformity to normal and expected patterns of behaviour. A role, to put it in more precise sociological terms, is 'a set of norms and expectations applied to the incumbents of a particular position' (Banton 1965: 29). The incumbents we are concerned with here are those who take up positions in the language class—teachers and pupils, or learners. The questions I now want to discuss are, what are the norms and expectations associated with these particular roles? And what particular positions do the incumbents occupy?

The classroom provides the context for the enactment of these roles: but the classroom should not just be perceived as physical surroundings but also conceived as social space. The difference is important and can be marked by a terminological distinction: *setting* for the physical context, *scene* for the socio-psychological one. These are terms and distinctions proposed by Hymes:

> Setting refers to the time and place of a speech act and, in general, to the physical circumstances. Scene, which is distinct from setting, designates the 'psychological setting', or the cultural definition of an occasion as a certain type of scene . . . In daily life the same persons in the same setting may redefine their interaction as a changed type of scene, say, from formal to informal, serious to festive, or the like.   *(1972: 60)*

Hymes identifies setting and scene as factors in the speech event, the situated communicative occurrence of language use. Since the classroom lesson is a type of speech event, it should be possible to characterize it in terms of these and the other factors which Hymes proposes.

With reference to setting, we might consider the physical features of the classroom which facilitate or constrain certain interactive procedures. If the walls are thin, this fact sets limits on activities which might provoke too much noise; if the desks are ranged in lines facing the teacher and fixed to the floor, this fact inhibits the setting up of small group discussion. So setting factors will have an influence on the kind of scene which the teacher wishes to create. One might compare the effect of seating arrangements in such places as courts of law or parliamentary assemblies.

But it is the socio-psychologically defined context, the scene, which is of particular relevance in recognizing how roles are assumed by classroom incumbents. The protagonists have to be in position both socially and physically before the scene is set and the play can begin. The teacher comes into the room. There is a lull in the hubbub, a transitional phase of settling down. Then: 'Right. Quiet please. Sit down.' The tumult and the shouting die. The scene is set. The classroom is constituted as a kind of social scene and the lesson starts. The participants, or the players, assume their normal and expected positions.

But what are these positions exactly? We have names for them in English: '(school)master', '(school)mistress', 'teacher', on the one hand; 'pupil', 'student', 'learner', on the other. But the terms on each side are not in free variation: they seem to suggest different things, conjure up different images. And this gives some indication, I think, that the roles of the classroom protagonists are not as straightforward as they might at first appear.

Let us look first at the terms 'pupil' and 'student'. These denote stable and socially established roles at different stages of life (studenthood in Britain seems to coincide roughly with the right to vote) and they are institutionalized and a part of the incumbent's identity. So the terms can be used to mark social categories and to specify occupation. Someone might say, in a conversation, 'Rupert, you know, is a student at Oxford', or we might read as a newspaper item 'Fiona Chetwynd, a pupil at The Priory School, is the new junior East Basingstoke badminton champion.' But people are not categorized or identified as *learners*. Being a learner is not an occupation but an incidental activity. The term denotes a role of temporary engagement which does not attach to the incumbent as a continuing characteristic: it is not a means of identification. We cannot say that Rupert is a learner at Oxford or Fiona a learner at The Priory School. And, by the same token, we have a National Union of Students but not a National Union of Learners. Learners are not kinds of people. Students and pupils are. You can be a learner whenever you like; you do not have to formalize your position.

In Britain, though, we do have a National Union of Teachers. This, together with the fact that this is the same sort of organization as the National Association of *Schoolmasters* and Women *Teachers*, indicates that the term 'teacher' is ambiguous. It can be used to refer to an identifying and categorizing role, in which case it is synonymous with '(school)master' and '(school)mistress', and corresponds to the terms 'pupil' and 'student'. But it can also be used in reference to a temporary and incidental role, which is engaged as an activity as and when occasion requires, and in this case it corresponds to the term 'learner'.

What I am suggesting, then, is that we find two really quite different kinds of role enacted in the classroom. One has to do with occupation and is identifying (pupil, student; master, mistress) and the other kind has to do with activity and is incidental (learner), with the term 'teacher' ambiguous, able to denote both. Now it happens that, as with other things, they order this matter better in France. The terms *professeur, écolier* and *étudiant(e)* denote the identifying occupational roles, the terms *enseignant(e)* and *apprenant(e)* the incidental activity ones.

Two kinds of classroom engagement

Well, this may or may not be of interest, but how is it relevant? It would seem to me that what this distinction suggests is that the classroom encounter is compounded of two kinds of engagement. These sometimes converge and sometimes conflict, and it seems to me that it is of central concern for classroom methodology to get these two kinds of engagement to synchronize effectively.

One kind of engagement involves the identifying roles: the teacher as *professeur* (master or mistress) in some sort of social interaction with the pupil. This let us call an *interactional* engagement. The norms and expectations defining appropriate behaviour here will be very much a matter of social attitude and educational ideology. This kind of engagement is a microcosmic school version of the macrocosm of social life and reflects the way educationists believe pupils should be socialized. It services the hidden curriculum of acculturation and the promotion of accepted values. It is the mode of interaction itself which is intended to have the principal educational effect.

But the classroom also has what we might call a *transactional* purpose—that is to say, it is meant to meet certain explicit learning objectives, to instigate activities directed at achieving specified goals. Here what I have called the incidental roles are brought into play: teacher as teaching person (*enseignant*) on the one hand, learner (*apprenant*) on the other. The norms and expectations here relate to pedagogic purpose: ways of defining roles which are likely to be the most effective for dealing with a particular subject on the *overt* curriculum, for developing specified knowledge and skills, for meeting the demands of the examination.

The two kinds of engagement and their different role realizations can of course key in with each other in a convenient and complementary way, with a particular kind of interaction facilitating a particular kind of transaction, educational and pedagogic perspectives nicely converging into a single focus. But it can also happen that they are at variance. Proposals for change in one kind of engagement can conflict with the conventions which characterize the other. A rationale for one kind of engagement can be mistakenly supposed to apply with equal validity to the other.

With this in mind, consider the following example of a type of classroom interaction. The teacher is accorded high status and commands deference. This might be symbolized by dress: formal clothing (a jacket and a tie for a man) or perhaps even an academic gown. There is protocol to be observed: pupils fall silent when the teacher enters the room, they stand up and chant a choral greeting. One of their number cleans the board. There are ritualistic practices to be strictly adhered to. Pupils are addressed by their surnames, the teacher by title (Mrs A, Mr B). The interaction itself is tightly controlled. Only the teacher has the right to initiate exchanges. Pupils can only contribute when they make a bid by raising the hand and when this is acknowledged and ratified as a claim for a speaking turn. Only one pupil speaks at once. The teacher only asks questions to which he or she already knows the answers. The rights and obligations associated with the teacher and pupil roles are clear, fixed and non-negotiable. They are established by 'norms of interaction', another of Hymes's factors, which he defines as 'specific behaviours and properties that attach to speaking —that one must not interrupt, for example, or that one may freely do so . . . that turns in speaking are to be allocated in a certain way'. (1972: 63–4)

Now one may think that this kind of interactional engagement is just a quaint and rather Dickensian remnant of the past, to be dismissed out of hand and clearly to be condemned as bad practice. But on what grounds?

Well, we might invoke a more enlightened ideology and say that the kind of education promoted by this type of interaction is one which forces the individual into conformity with existing patterns of power, schools the pupils into maintaining an iniquitious social structure which favours a self-appointed elite and effectively acts as an instrument of disenfranchisement. The pupils are put in this position in the classroom so that they can be more effectively kept in their place in social life. We may indeed, as many others have done, challenge the idea that there needs to be any clear definition of role at all. We may wish to think of the classroom engagement as being not a position-oriented but a person-oriented interaction (to use Bernstein's distinction, see Chapter 9) and so get rid of all this cumbersome ritual. No sartorial signs of office, no gown, no suit or tie—just a sweatshirt and sneakers. No position and no imposition. 'Don't call me Sir. Don't call me Mr Brown. Call me Dave.' 'Don't call me Miss. Don't call me Miss Brown. Call me Liz.' Equal opportunities and human rights . . .

So we might object to the traditional interaction I have presented on the ideological grounds that it runs counter to enlightened educational thinking. It is fundamentally undemocratic. But we could also object to it on more expedient and practical grounds by saying that, whatever the moral or political or social objections might be, such an interaction is to be proscribed because it is inconsistent with the kind of pedagogic transaction needed to facilitate language learning. It just does not create the right sort of enabling conditions. Now this is a very different sort of objection and needs different arguments to sustain it.

It might be pointed out, for example, that such a rigid definition of role impedes the natural learning process since it does not allow for learner initiatives: it does not give the learner scope to draw on the available resources of intuition and inventiveness, or to engage freely the procedures for learning which he or she has acquired through a previous experience of language. Nor does such a role definition allow for the provision of group work (see Brumfit 1984a: Chapter 5; Wright 1987: Section 2.3). A teaching role which determines learner activity by directing it radially, so to speak, from the pedagogic podium is, of course, based on the assumption that learners can only learn from approved and appointed teachers and not from each other. Thus the collective potential that learners bring to class as a resource for learning is left unexploited. We might adduce evidence from research on the 'Good Language Learner' (see, for example, Naiman *et al.* 1978) and on natural second language acquisition (see Ellis 1985) in support of the contention that such a close adherence to fixed prescribed roles in the classroom is detrimental to effective (and affective) learning.

Now these are points which bear on pedagogic and not educational issues. They concern the optimal conditions for learning. The interaction in this case is evaluated not in its own social terms but in reference to its degree of congruence with a preferred type of pedagogic *transaction*.

It is not always easy to keep these two kinds of classroom engagement distinct. One is tempted to suppose that if a particular role-relationship between teacher and learners is transactionally effective in one set of circumstances then it will transfer (and should be transferred) to others. But the effectiveness may depend on a particular interactional role-relationship between teacher and pupil which is simply not sanctioned as educationally desirable in a different social situation. A humanistic, group therapy approach to pedagogy may be highly effective (and affectively highly enjoyable) in places which favour person-oriented education, but impossible to implement in places where different educational ideology calls for a very different kind of interactional engagement in class, one based on clear positional definition established by tradition. Again, it is tempting to believe that if a particular concept of interaction has an especially appealing ideological ring to it, then it must needs be transactionally effective; that setting pupils free of their traditionally ascribed roles, for example, will as a corollary make them better learners. But this, of course, does not follow at all. If there is a causal relationship, then it needs to be demonstrated. It cannot just be taken on trust, or on faith, or confirmed by the fiat of ideological commitment.

Teacher authority and learner autonomy

This dual functioning of the classroom encounter that I have briefly outlined has a bearing on two related issues which are prominent in present debate in our profession, and which make their appearance, in various guises, in many conference programmes. One of these is teacher authority. The other is learner autonomy.

Challenging authority in general is a popular activity at present in those societies where the populace has the liberty to do so. In education, the teacher as *professeur* has come under some suspicion as a possible agent of authority which seeks to maintain the power of privilege, schooling pupils into obedient compliance. In pedagogy (or in our branch of it at least) the view in vogue among those who claim expertise seems increasingly to be that expressed nearly two thousand years ago by Cicero: 'Most commonly the authority of them that teach hinders them that would learn.'

But I think it is important to realize that the exercise of

authority in interaction is different from the exercise of authority in transaction, as I have defined those terms.

In interaction, the teacher—as *professeur*—claims a superior and dominant position by virtue of a role which has been socially ascribed to him or her: 'I am your teacher. By the authority vested in me I have the right to ask you to behave in a certain way, whether you like it or not. And you, in your role, have the obligation to obey.' So the exercise of authority in interaction is more or less authoritarian.

But the teacher as *enseignant* exercises authority in trans-action by virtue of the achieved role of expert. His or her authority is based on professional qualification. Dominance derives from the claim to be able to teach, to make the transaction successful in respect of its specified objectives. In this case there is no assertion of right but a claim to knowledge: not 'Do this because I tell you and I am the teacher' but 'Do this because I am the teacher and I know what's best for you.' Transactional exercise of authority, therefore, is more or less authoritative.

This difference between being authoritarian and authoritative is nicely illustrated in a recently published paper by Barry Taylor. He argues for the need to foster 'self-investment' and whole-person goal accomplishment as a condition for effective learning through engagement with communicative tasks. Such an approach, he says,

> points at *the need to maintain a non-authoritarian presence* throughout this process so that students can feel secure and non-defensive to enable them to learn not because the teacher demands it of them, but because they need to in order to accomplish their own goals.

But then he goes on in the next paragraph:

> This approach stresses that sharing the responsibility for structuring learning with the students does not require that teachers abdicate *their fundamental* authority to guide and structure their classes.   *(1987: 58 [my italics])*

How we view the exercise of authority in interaction will depend on our attitude to education and the society it serves. The ideological trend in the western world is towards a less authoritarian position and perhaps this is indeed necessary for the maintenance of an open society. Be that as it may, this is a quite different issue from the exercise of authority in transaction. For no matter how we view pedagogy, no matter how much initiative we believe should be allowed to the learner, the teacher as *enseignant* must surely retain an undiminished authority. The increase in learner-centred activity and collaborative work in the classroom does not mean that the teacher becomes less authoritative. He or she still has to contrive the required enabling conditions for learning, still has to monitor and guide progress.

And all this presupposes an expertise, applied perhaps with more subtlety and consideration and discretion than before, but applied none the less. I see no future whatever for any pedagogy which undermines the authority of the teacher in his or her role as *enseignant*, as ultimately responsible for the management of classroom transactions. Indeed, if one does *not* allow the legitimacy of this authority, then I do not see any point in talking about pedagogy at all. It seems to me that it is because these differences in the exercise of authority have not been properly recognized that the authoritative actions of the teacher have at times been discredited quite improperly as authoritarian impositions of power.

Finally, a word about learner autonomy. This too has its transactional and interactional aspects. As far as the transactional aspect is concerned, the learner (*apprenant*) really only exercises autonomy within the limits set by teacher authority. The learner is never really independent, it is the *kind* of dependency which changes.

A distinction is commonly made between the natural contexts of learning which allow for the exercise of independence and the contrived contexts of instruction which enforce constraints. The first are associated with the primary socialization of family and friends, and the second with the secondary socialization of the school. But the distinction can be too starkly drawn. In upbringing the child is subject to all manner of controls and is constrained to conform to established patterns of behaviour whether these are determined by members of the family or peer group. Those in contact with the child contrive to shape its behaviour and there can be penalties for nonconformity at least as disagreeable as those devised by the school. Indeed one might define the very concept of learning in general as the recognition of appropriate authority.

So the idea of 'natural' learning as being a process of untrammelled discovery or self-directed quest seems to me to be misleading. The process is always directed. The issue is not whether or not it should be subjected to direction, because it always is, but what *kind* of direction is most ideologically desirable and most pedagogically effective. This is not to deny the possibility that there are certain parameters of language development which are innately programmed in the mind. However, the fixing of these parameters in the learning of particular languages is, I suggest, always dependent on the action of external control of one kind or another, applied with varying degrees of indirectness and subtlety.

Learner autonomy in the transaction of language learning is therefore necessarily restricted. And it is interesting to note that when *interactional* autonomy is given the opportunity to assert itself, it can have consequences which run counter to trans-actional purposes. Consider again, for example, the case of group work.

The teacher may arrange for the class to work, let us say, on problem-solving tasks in groups. From a transactional point of view, this has the advantage of increasing participation in the use and practice of language (see Long and Porter 1985). But if the groups are to operate by exercising *interactional* autonomy in an independent and unconstrained way then they will quite naturally develop their own norms and expectations and these will apply not to the role of pupil at all but to the role of peer group member.

The crucial point here is that there are in fact two separate interaction groups in a classroom. One of them is overt and consists of the teacher as *professeur* and the collectivity of pupils. The other is covert for most of the time and consists of the children themselves within their own peer group, where the criteria for pupilhood no longer apply. It is this other group which is in interactive operation in the hubbub before the teacher comes in to set the scene and start the lesson. This group then, as it were, goes underground, only surfacing from time to time, often with disruptive effects. Now this group of course has its own social norms and these have little correspondence with those of the pupil. It has its own standards of appropriate behaviour and these are not likely to match up with what the teacher expects from group activity. Thus the group may see it as appropriate in reference to *their* norms of behaviour to withdraw commitment, to sabotage the activity, to ridicule attempts to use the foreign language and to give high prestige to comic incorrectness and impropriety. There are, then, obvious dangers in allowing groups to exercise a genuine *interactional* autonomy. This should not be taken as a recommendation that all interactional autonomy should be suppressed, but only that it should be subject to careful consideration lest an ideological zeal for democratic gesture should undermine the whole pedagogic enterprise.

I believe that the success of this enterprise, to which we are all presumably committed, depends on our recognizing and resolving the difficulties inherent in the dual functioning of roles in the classroom encounter that I have outlined, and on a reconciliation of the claims of authority of the teacher on the one hand, and the claims of autonomy of learner and pupil on the other. As in other areas of social life, success in transaction and interaction in the classroom depends on our knowing the parts we have to play and how they relate with those that others enact in the encounters in which we are engaged.

Conclusion

Chapter 11 ended with a consideration of the relationship between teacher authority and learner autonomy. The central question this poses is: how can learner behaviour be delimited in such a way as to direct initiative towards the achievement of effective learning? We have come full circle to the issue to which I referred in Chapter 1, namely the need to acknowledge that individual enterprise can only be meaningful if it is bounded. Creativity is only possible in reference to established convention. Freedom presupposes restriction. All the chapters in this book can be read as variations on this basic theme. The activities of language users, language teachers, and language learners can all be characterized as ways of achieving particular purposes by reference to a general conceptual framework which at the same time delimits these activities and defines their significance.

Put simply, the proposition is that all new experience is necessarily circumscribed by what is given. An absolute exercise of initiative, to the extent that this is possible at all, would result in confusion. In reference to language use, one cannot just use words and structures at random in the hope that context will somehow provide the necessary co-ordinates of meaning. Meanings are not freely negotiable. They are constrained by established rules and conventions: the rules of the language system, the conventions of their communicative use. But although they are constrained, they are not determined. There is always room for manoeuvre. Competence in language must be a matter of knowing these constraints and using them in association with context to narrow down the possibilities of meaning on actual occasions. These constraints, these rules and conventions are general variables which have to be given particular values.

These variables and values correspond to the principles and techniques of language teaching. Techniques are activities which are designed to meet the needs of a particular context, like linguistic utterances. But they also realize more general principles, just as the utterance realizes more general categories of linguistic and social knowledge no matter how closely it may be keyed in with the needs of the context. The ability to adjust linguistic behaviour contingently to meet particular communicative requirements presupposes a knowledge of general rules and conventions. In the same way, the ability to adjust techniques to account for the demands of different classroom contexts presupposes a knowledge of more general pedagogic principles. In other words, the pragmatics of language teaching discussed in Part 1 correspond with the pragmatics of language use discussed in Part 2.

What then of language learners? They, too, need some given conceptual framework within which to operate if their activities are to have any point. The central task of pedagogy is to find the framework which is most effective for learning. This will necessarily involve taking into account the attitudes, interests, and predispositions of the learners themselves. How far this calls for open consultation or negotiation with learners in the design of courses, how far this design is established as a projected plan or as a continuous process, are matters which can only be determined in reference to particular teaching/learning situations. But whatever process is most expedient, the end result must be a framework of some kind, some set of bearings to enable learners to find their way. It should also be borne in mind that whatever initiative learners are allowed, the destination will, in most cases, be determined by decisions beyond their control. This is one aspect of language learner behaviour which distinguishes it from that of normal language use: it is necessarily prescribed. The contexts in which it occurs are contrived for its inducement. One can disguise the contrivance, stimulate learner incentive and exploit learner initiative in all manner of ways. These are the usual tactics of teaching. But ultimately they serve the basic strategy of control. They are manoeuvres within confinement. We come here to another distinguishing feature of language learner behaviour. It is only valid to the extent that it induces knowledge, that is to say, that it leads the learner to extrapolate, to generalize beyond the immediate and particular circumstances of its occurrence. As we have seen, using a language already acquired is a matter of referring the particular to the general, but to acquire a language one needs to infer the general from the particular.

All this points to the conclusion that we should not assume

that language using behaviour is necessarily effective as language learning behaviour, or that natural learning potential once released from the inhibiting confinement of teacher control will lead learners to home in on their objectives. One does not solve the complex problems of language pedagogy by simply invoking the concepts of authenticity of language on the one hand, and the autonomy of learners on the other. There needs to be a continuing process of principled pragmatic enquiry. I offer this book as a contribution to this process—and as such, it can have no conclusion.

Bibliography

Alatis, J. E. (ed.). 1978. *International Dimensions of Bilingual Education*. Washington D.C.: Georgetown University Press.

Alatis, J. E., H. H. Stern, and D. Strevens (eds.). 1983. *Applied Linguistics and the Preparation of Second Language Teachers: Toward a Rationale*. Washington D. C.: Georgetown University Press.

Alderson, J. C. (ed.). 1985. 'Evaluation.' *Lancaster Papers in English Language Education* 6. Oxford: Pergamon.

Alderson, J. C. and A. H. Urquhart (eds.). 1984. *Reading in a Foreign Language*. London: Longman.

Allen, J. P. B. and P. van Buren (eds.). 1971. *Chomsky: Selected Readings*. London: Oxford University Press.

Allen, J. P. B. and H. G. Widdowson. 1973. *English in Physical Science*. London: Oxford University Press.

Allwright, R. L. 1983. 'Classroom centred research in language teaching and learning: A brief historical review.' *TESOL Quarterly* 17/2.

Allwright, R. L. 1988. *Observation in the Language Classroom*. London: Longman.

Anderson, A. and T. Lynch. 1988. *Listening*. Oxford: Oxford University Press.

Asher, J. 1982. *Learning Another Language Through Actions: The Complete Teacher's Guide Book* (2nd edition). Los Gatos, CA: Sky Oaks Publications.

Aston, G. 1986. 'Trouble-shooting in interaction with learners: the more the merrier?' *Applied Linguistics* 7/2.

Bachman, L. 1990. *Fundamental Considerations in Language Testing*. Oxford: Oxford University Press.

Banton, M. 1965. *Roles: An Introduction to the Study of Social Relations*. London: Tavistock Publications.

Bernstein, B. B. 1971. *Class, Codes and Control* 1. London: Routledge and Kegan Paul.

Bialystok, E. 1982. 'On the relationship between knowing and using linguistic forms.' *Applied Linguistics* 3/3.

Bialystok, E. and M. Sharwood-Smith. 1985. 'Interlanguage is not a state of mind: an evaluation of the construct for second language acquisition.' *Applied Linguistics* 6/2.

Bolinger, D. 1976. 'Meaning and memory.' *Forum Linguisticum* 1/1.

Breen, M. P. 1985. 'Authenticity in the language classroom.' *Applied Linguistics* 6/1.

Breen, M. P. 1987. 'Contemporary paradigms in syllabus design.' *Language Teaching* 20/3, 4.

Breen, M. P. and C. N. Candlin. 1980. 'The essentials of a communicative curriculum in language teaching.' *Applied Linguistics* 1/2.

Breen, M. P., C. N. Candlin, L. Dam, and G. Gabrielson. 1988. 'The evolution of a teacher training programme' in Johnson, (ed.) 1988.

Brown, G. and G. Yule. 1983. *Discourse Analysis*. Cambridge: Cambridge University Press.

Brown, P. and S. Levinson. 1978. 'Universals in language usage: politeness phenomena' in Goody (ed.) 1978.

Brumfit, A. and S. Windeatt. 1984. *Communicative Grammar 2 and 3*. Beirut/Oxford: English Language Teaching for the Arab World/Oxford University Press SARL.

Brumfit, C. J. 1983. 'The integration of theory and practice' in Alatis *et al.* (eds.) 1983.

Brumfit, C. J. 1984a. *Communicative Methodology in Language Teaching: the Roles of Fluency and Accuracy*. Cambridge: Cambridge University Press.

Brumfit, C. J. 1984b. 'The Bangalore Procedural Syllabus.' *English Language Teaching Journal* 38/4.

Brumfit, C. J. 1984c. 'Theoretical implications of Interlanguage studies for language teaching' in Davies *et al.* (eds.) 1984.

Brumfit, C. J. (ed.). 1984d. *General English Syllabus Design*. Oxford: Pergamon.

Brumfit, C. J. 1985. *Language and Literature Teaching: From Practice to Principle*. Oxford: Pergamon.

Brumfit, C. J. (ed.). 1986. *The Practice of Communicative Language Teaching*. Oxford: Pergamon.

Brumfit, C. J. 1987. 'Concepts and categories in language teaching methodology' in Kuhlwein (ed.) 1987.

Brumfit, C. J. and **R. A. Carter** (eds.). 1986. *Literature and Language Teaching*. Oxford: Oxford University Press.

Brumfit, C. J. and **K. Johnson** (eds.). 1979. *The Communicative Approach to Language Teaching*. Oxford: Oxford University Press.

Burt, M., H. Dulay, and **E. Hernandez.** 1973. *Bilingual Syntax Measure*. New York: Harcourt Brace Jovanovich.

Bygate, M. 1987. *Speaking*. Oxford: Oxford University Press.

Canale, M. and **M. Swain.** 1980. 'Theoretical bases of communicative approaches to language teaching and testing.' *Applied Linguistics* 1/1.

Candlin, C. N. 1983. 'Principles and problems for INSET in implementing a communicative curriculum' in Alatis *et al.* (eds.) 1983.

Candlin, C. N. 1984. 'Syllabus design as critical process' in Brumfit (ed.) 1984c.

Candlin, C. N. 1985. 'Teacher-centred training: costing the process' in Quirk and Widdowson (eds.) 1985.

Candlin, C. N. and **H. G. Widdowson** (eds.). 1987. *Language Teaching: A Scheme for Teacher Education*. Oxford: Oxford University Press.

Carrell, P. 1983. 'Some issues in the role of schemata, or background knowledge, in second language comprehension.' *Reading in a Foreign Language* 1/2.

Carrell, P. 1987. 'Content and formal schemata in ESL reading.' *TESOL Quarterly* 21/3.

Carter R. and **M. McCarthy** (eds.), 1988. *Vocabulary and Language Teaching*. London: Longman.

Chomsky, N. 1959. Review of *Verbal Behaviour* by B. F. Skinner. *Language* 35.

Chomsky, N. 1965. *Aspects of the Theory of Syntax*. Cambridge, Mass.: MIT Press.

Chomsky, N. 1980. *Rules and Representations*. Oxford: Blackwell.

Clark, J. L. 1987. *Curriculum Renewal in School Foreign Language Teaching*. Oxford: Oxford University Press.

Coates, J. 1982. *The Semantics of the Modal Auxiliaries*. London: Croom Helm.

Cole, P. and **J. Morgan** (eds.). 1975. *Syntax and Semantics 3: Speech Acts*. New York: Academic Press.

Collins COBUILD English Language Dictionary. 1987. London and Glasgow: Collins.

Cook, G. 1989. *Discourse.* Oxford: Oxford University Press.

Cook, V. J. 1983. 'What should language teaching be about?' *English Language Teaching Journal* 37/3.

Corder, S. P. 1973. *Introducing Applied Linguistics.* Harmondsworth: Penguin Books.

Corder, S. P. 1981. *Error Analysis and Interlanguage.* Oxford: Oxford University Press.

Coulmas, F. 1981. *Festschift for Native Speaker.* The Hague: Mouton.

Coulthard, R. M. (ed.). 1986. *Talking about Text.* English Language Research: University of Birmingham.

Cowie, A. P. 1988. 'Stable and creative aspects of vocabulary use' in Carter and McCarthy (eds.) 1988.

Crombie, W. 1985. *Discourse and Language Learning: A Relational Approach to Syllabus Design.* Oxford: Oxford University Press.

Crystal, D. 1980. *A First Dictionary of Linguistics and Phonetics.* London: Andre Deutsch.

Dakin, J. 1973. *The Language Laboratory and Language Learning.* London: Longman.

Dakin, J., B. Tiffen, and H. G. Widdowson. 1968. *Language in Education.* London: Oxford University Press.

Davies, A., C. Criper, and A. P. R. Howatt (eds.). 1984. *Interlanguage.* Edinburgh: Edinburgh University Press.

Donaldson, M. 1978. *Children's Minds.* Glasgow: Collins/Fontana.

Edelhoff, C. 1983. 'Putting the communicative curriculum into practice: the organization of teacher in-service education and training in Hesse, Germany' in Alatis *et al.* (eds.) 1983.

Edelhoff, C. 1985. 'A view from teacher in-service education and training' in Quirk and Widdowson (eds.) 1985.

Elliott, G. 1981. *Self-Evaluation and the Teacher.* London: Schools Council.

Ellis, R. 1985. *Understanding Second Language Acquisition.* Oxford: Oxford University Press.

Færch C. and G. Kasper (eds.). 1985. 'Foreign language learning under classroom conditions.' *Studies in Second Language Acquisition* (Special Issue) 2/2.

Firth, J. R. 1957. *Papers in Linguistics 1934–1951*. London: Oxford University Press.

Gleason, J. B. 1982. 'Converging evidence for linguistic theory from the study of aphasia and child language' in Obler and Menn (eds.) 1982.

Goffman, E. 1974. *Frame Analysis*. New York: Harper and Row.

Goody, E. (ed.). 1978. *Questions and Politeness. Strategies in Social Interaction*. Cambridge: Cambridge University Press.

Gregg, K. 1984. 'Krashen's monitor and Occam's razor.' *Applied Linguistics* 5/2.

Grice, H. P. 1975. 'Logic and conversation' in Cole and Morgan (eds.) 1975.

Hakuta, K. 1974. 'Emergence of structure in second language acquisition.' *Language Learning* 24.

Halliday, M. A. K. 1985. *An Introduction to Functional Grammar*. London: Edward Arnold.

Halliday, M. A. K., A. McIntosh, and P. Strevens. 1964. *The Linguistic Sciences and Language Teaching*. London: Longman.

Harley, B. and M. Swain. 1984. 'The interlanguage of immersion students and its implications for second language learning' in Davies *et al.* (eds.) 1984.

Hartford, B., A. Valdman, and C. R. Foster (eds.). 1982. *Issues in International Bilingual Education*. New York: Plenum Press.

Hatch, E. 1979. 'Apply with caution.' *Studies in Second Language Acquisition* 2/1.

Hornby, A. S. (ed.) 1946. *English Language Teaching* 1/1.

Hudson, R. A. 1980. *Sociolinguistics*. Cambridge: Cambridge University Press.

Hymes, D. 1972. 'On communicative competence' in Pride and Holmes (eds.) 1972.

Johnson, K. 1979. 'Communicative approaches and communicative processes' in Brumfit and Johnson (eds.) 1979.

Johnson, K. 1982. *Communicative Syllabus Design and Methodology*. Oxford: Pergamon.

Johnson, K. (ed.). 1988. *Programme Design and Evaluation in Language Teaching.* Cambridge: Cambridge University Press.

Johnson-Laird, P. N. 1983. *Mental Models.* Cambridge: Cambridge University Press.

Krashen, S. D. 1981. *Second Language Acquisition and Second Language Learning.* Oxford: Pergamon.

Krashen, S. D. 1982. 'The fundamental pedagogical principle in second language teaching.' *Studia Linguistica* 35/1, 2.

Krashen, S. D. 1983. 'Second language acquisition theory and the preparation of teachers: towards a rationale' in Alatis *et al.* (eds.) 1983.

Krashen, S. D. and **T. Terrell.** 1983. *The Natural Approach.* Oxford: Pergamon.

Kuhlwein, W. (ed.). 1987. 'Linguistics in Applied Linguistics.' *AILA Review* 4.

Labov, W. 1984. 'Intensity' in Schiffrin (ed.) 1984.

Lado, R. and **C. C. Fries.** 1957. *An Intensive Course in English.* Michigan: University of Michigan Press.

Larsen-Freeman, D. 1983. 'Training teachers or educating a teacher?' in Alatis *et al.* (eds.) 1983.

Leech, G. N. 1983. *Principles of Pragmatics.* London: Longman.

Levinson, S. N. 1983. *Pragmatics.* Cambridge: Cambridge University Press.

Levinson, S. N. 1987. 'Pragmatics and the grammar of anaphora: a partial pragmatic reduction of binding and control phenomena.' *Journal of Linguistics* 23/2.

van Lier, L. 1988. *The Classroom and the Language Learner.* London: Longman.

Long, M. H. 1983a. 'Native speaker/non-native speaker conversation and the negotiation of comprehensible input.' *Applied Linguistics* 4/2.

Long, M. H. 1983b. 'Training the language teacher as researcher' in Alatis *et al.* (eds.) 1983.

Long, M. H. 1983c. 'Inside the "Black Box": methodological issues in classroom research on language learning' in Seliger and Long (eds.) 1983.

Long, M. H. 1985. 'A role for instruction in second language acquisition' in Pienemann and Hyltenstam (eds.) 1985.

Long, M. H. and **P. A. Porter.** 1985. 'Group work, interlanguage talk, and second language acquisition.' TESOL Quarterly 19/2.

Long, M. H. and **J. C. Richards** (eds.). 1987. *Methodology in TESOL: A Book of Readings.* New York: Newbury House.

Mackey, W. F. 1965. *Language Teaching Analysis.* London: Longman.

McLaughlin, B. 1978. 'The Monitor Model: some methodological considerations.' *Language Learning* 28/3.

McLaughlin, B. 1987. *Theories in Second Language Learning.* London: Edward Arnold.

Malamah-Thomas, A. 1987. *Classroom Interaction.* Oxford: Oxford University Press.

Mitchell, R. 1985. 'Process research in second language classrooms.' *Language Teaching* 18/4.

Morrison, D. M. and **G. Low.** 1983. 'Monitoring and the second language learner' in Richards and Schmidt (eds.) 1983.

Moskowitz, G. 1978. *Caring and Sharing in the Foreign Language Classroom.* Rowley, Mass.: Newbury House.

Murphy, D. F. 1985. 'Evaluation in language teaching: assessment, accountability and awareness' in Alderson (ed.) 1985.

Naiman, N., M. Fröhlich, and **H. H. Stern.** 1978. *The Good Language Learner.* Toronto: OISE.

Nattinger, J. 1988. 'Some current trends in vocabulary teaching' in Carter and McCarthy (eds.) 1988.

Newmeyer, F. J. 1983. *Grammatical Theory: Its Limitations and Possibilities.* Chicago: University of Chicago Press.

Nunan, D. 1988. *Syllabus Design.* Oxford: Oxford University Press.

Obler, L. K. and **L. Menn** (eds.). 1982. *Exceptional Language and Linguistics.* New York: Academic Press.

Olson, D. R. 1981. 'The literate native speaker: some intellectual consequences of the language of schooling' in Coulmas 1981.

Palmer, F. R. 1981. *Semantics.* Cambridge: Cambridge University Press.

Pawley, A. and **F. Syder.** 1983. 'Two puzzles for linguistic theory: native-like selection and native-like fluency' in Richards and Schmidt (eds.) 1983.

Peters, A. M. 1983. *The Units of Language Acquisition.* Cambridge: Cambridge University Press.

Peters, R. S. 1967. *The Concept of Education.* London: Routledge and Kegan Paul.

Peters, R. S. (ed.). 1983. *The Philosophy of Education.* London: Oxford University Press.

Piaget, J. 1955. *The Child's Construction of Reality.* London: Routledge and Kegan Paul.

Pienemann, M. 1985. 'Learnability and syllabus construction' in Pienemann and Hyltenstam (eds.) 1985.

Pienemann, M. and K. Hyltenstam (eds.). 1985. *Modelling and Assessing Second Language Acquisition.* Clevedon: Multi-lingual Matters.

Prabhu, N. S. 1985. 'Coping with the unknown in language pedagogy' in Quirk and Widdowson (eds.) 1985.

Prabhu, N. S. 1987. *Second Language Pedagogy.* Oxford: Oxford University Press.

Pride, J. B. and J. Holmes (eds.). 1972. *Sociolinguistics: Selected Readings.* Harmondsworth: Penguin Books.

Quirk, R., S. Greenbaum, G. N. Leech, and J. Svartvik. 1972. *A Grammar of Contemporary English.* London: Longman.

Quirk, R., S. Greenbaum, G. N. Leech, and J. Svartvik. 1985. *A Comprehensive Grammar of the English Language.* London: Longman.

Quirk, R. and H. G. Widdowson (eds.). 1985. *English in the World.* Cambridge: Cambridge University Press.

Richards, J. C. and R. W. Schmidt (eds.). 1983. *Language and Communication.* London: Longman.

Richards, J. C., H. Weber, and J. Platt (eds.). 1984. *The Longman Dictionary of Applied Linguistics.* London: Longman.

Rivers, W. 1964. *The Psychologist and the Foreign Language Teacher.* Chicago: University of Chicago Press.

Rogers, C. 1969. *Freedom to Learn.* Ohio: Charles E. Merrill.

Rubin, J. 1975. 'What the "Good Language Learner" can teach us.' *TESOL Quarterly* 9/1.

Rubin, J. 1981. 'Study of cognitive processes in language learning.' *Applied Linguistics* 2/2.

Rutherford, W. 1987. *Second Language Grammar: Learning and Teaching.* London: Longman.

Rutherford, W. and M. Sharwood-Smith. 1988. *Grammar and Second Language Teaching*. New York: Newbury House.

Sampson, G. 1980. *Schools of Linguistics*. London: Hutchinson.

Schiffrin, D. (ed.). 1984. *Meaning, Form, and Use in Context: Linguistic Applications*. Washington D. C.: Georgetown University Press.

Scriven, M. 1967. 'The methodology of evaluation' in Tyler *et al.* 1967.

Seliger, H. W. and M. H. Long (eds.). 1983. *Classroom Oriented Research in Second Language Acquisition*. Rowley, Mass.: Newbury House.

Selinker, L. 1984. 'The current state of Interlanguage studies: an attempted critical summary' in Davies *et al.* (eds.) 1984.

Selinker, L. and D. Douglas. 1985. 'Wrestling with "context" in Interlanguage theory.' *Applied Linguistics* 6/2.

Sharwood-Smith, M. 1981. 'Consciousness-raising and the second language learner.' *Applied Linguistics* 2/2.

Sinclair, J. M. 1985. 'Selected Issues' in Quirk and Widdowson (eds.) 1985.

Sinclair, J. M. and R. M. Coulthard. 1975. *Towards an Analysis of Discourse*. Oxford: Oxford University Press

Smith, P. 1970. *A Comparison of the Cognitive and Audiolingual Approaches to Foreign Language Instruction: The Pennsylvania Foreign Language Project*. Philadelphia: Center for Curriculum Development.

Spada, N. 1985. 'Some effects of the interaction between type of contact and instruction on the L2 proficiency of adult learners.' *Studies in Second Language Acquisition* 7/1.

Spada, N. 1987. 'Relationships between instructional differences and learning outcomes: A process-product study of communicative language teaching.' *Applied Linguistics* 8/2.

Sperber, D. and D. Wilson. 1986. *Relevance: Communication and Cognition*. Oxford: Basil Blackwell.

Stenhouse, L. 1975. *An Introduction to Curriculum Research and Development*. London: Heinemann Educational.

Stern, H. H. 1978. 'French immersion in Canada: achievements and directions.' *Canadian Modern Language Review* 34.

Stern, H. H. 1983. *Fundamental Concepts of Language Teaching*. Oxford: Oxford University Press.

Stern, H. H. 1984. 'Review and discussion' in Brumfit (ed.) 1984c.

Stubbs, M. 1986a. 'A matter of prolonged field work: notes towards a modal grammar of English.' *Applied Linguistics* 7/1.

Stubbs, M. 1986b. 'Lexical density: a computational technique and some findings' in Coulthard (ed.) 1986.

Swain, M. 1978. 'Bilingual education for the English-speaking Canadian' in Alatis (ed.) 1978.

Swain, M. 1982. 'Immersion education applicability for non-vernacular teaching to vernacular speakers' in Hartford *et al.* (eds.) 1982.

Swain, M. and **S. Lapkin.** 1981. *Bilingual Education: A Decade of Research.* Toronto: Ontario Ministry of Education.

Tarone, E. 1983. 'On the variability of Interlanguage systems.' *Applied Linguistics* 4/2.

Tarone, E. 1988. *Variation in Interlanguage.* London: Edward Arnold.

Taylor, B. 1987. 'Teaching ESL: incorporating a communicative, student-centred component' in Long and Richards (eds.) 1987.

Tickoo, M. L. (ed.). 1987. *Language Syllabuses: The State of the Art.* Singapore: RELC.

Todd, L. 1974. *Pidgins and Creoles.* London: Routledge and Kegan Paul.

Trim, J. L. M., R. Richterich, J. A. van Ek, and **D. A. Wilkins.** 1980. *Systems Development in Adult Language Learning: A European Unit/Credit System for Modern Language Learning by Adults.* The Council of Europe/Oxford: Pergamon.

Trimble, L. 1985. *English for Science and Technology.* Cambridge: Cambridge University Press.

Tyler, R., R. Gagne, and **M. Scriven.** 1967. *Perspectives of Curriculum Evaluation.* Chicago: Rand McNally.

Vihman, M. M. 1982. 'Formulas in first and second language acquisition' in Obler and Menn (eds.) 1982.

White, L. 1987. 'Against comprehensible input: the input hypothesis and the development of second language competence.' *Applied Linguistics* 8/2.

Widdowson, H. G. 1968. 'The teaching of English through Science' in Dakin *et al.* 1968.

Widdowson, H. G. 1975. *Stylistics and the Teaching of Literature*. London: Longman.

Widdowson, H. G. 1978. *Teaching Language as Communication*. Oxford: Oxford University Press.

Widdowson, H. G. 1979. *Explorations in Applied Linguistics*. Oxford: Oxford University Press.

Widdowson, H. G. 1983. *Learning Purpose and Language Use*. Oxford: Oxford University Press.

Widdowson, H. G. 1984a. *Explorations in Applied Linguistics 2*. Oxford: Oxford University Press.

Widdowson, H. G. 1984b. 'The incentive value of theory in teacher education.' *English Language Teaching Journal* 39/2.

Widdowson, H. G. 1985. 'The teaching, learning and study of literature' in Quirk and Widdowson (eds.) 1985.

Widdowson, H. G. 1989. 'Knowledge of language and ability for use.' *Applied Linguistics* 10/2.

Wilkins, D. A. 1976. *Notional Syllabuses*. London: Oxford University Press.

Wilkins, D. A. 1981. 'Notional syllabuses revisited.' *Applied Linguistics* 2/1.

Wright, T. 1987. *The Roles of Teacher and Learner*. Oxford: Oxford University Press.

Yule, G. 1985. *The Study of Language: An Introduction*. Cambridge: Cambridge University Press.

Index